D1366714

DREAM BOLD,
START SMART

— TATIANA TSOIR —

DREAM
BOLD

**BE YOUR OWN BOSS &
MAKE MONEY DOING
WHAT YOU LOVE**

START
SMART

PAGE TWO
BOOKS

Cataloguing in publication information is
available from Library and Archives Canada.
ISBN 978-1-77458-003-5 (hardcover)
ISBN 978-1-77458-030-1 (ebook)

Page Two
www.pagetwo.com

Edited by James Harbeck
Copyedited by Kendra Ward
Proofread by Alison Strobel
Cover and interior design by Taysia Louie
Interior illustrations by Michelle Clement
Printed and bound in Canada by Friesens
Distributed in Canada by Raincoast Books
Distributed in the US and internationally by
Publishers Group West, a division of Ingram

21 22 23 24 25 5 4 3 2 1

tatianatsoir.com
dreamboldbook.com

To my family, who tolerates my obsession with numbers and supports my passion every day.

Contents

Introduction

██████

SEVERAL YEARS AGO, we went to my daughter's friend's fourth birthday party. The kids spread out around the backyard, allowing the grown-ups to gather around food and alcohol and enjoy an adult conversation. The usual "what do you do for a living?" was thrown around a few times, and when it was my turn and I introduced myself as an accountant.

A few minutes later, as I was walking down the beautifully decorated hallway to check on my kids, one of the moms approached me and asked if I had a few minutes to talk. Her name was Amanda, she was in her late thirties, she had a calm demeanor but fidgeted a bit, and her eyes were glowing with hope: she was excited.

"I have this idea," she said. "I've always loved creating flower bouquets. It's something that speaks to me and I feel so happy when friends' faces light up with joy as they receive my creations on their special day. I was wondering: how do I make it, you know, a business or something, like, make money doing it?

"I want to stay flexible," she continued. "I want to be there for my kids but I would love to have some money, and, frankly, something that's just *mine*. I have no idea where to even begin and I am terrified of losing money."

So, we jumped on a call the next day and I outlined a few important decisions she needed to make as well as the steps she needed to complete to get her idea going.

People like Amanda approach me at every dang birthday party, wherever I go. They have passion and an idea, and are looking to me to tell them what to do, where to start, and, most importantly, how to make it work. And that may be the reason you are holding this book in your hands.

Maybe you don't have kids and have never been a stay-at-home mom but you've always been passionate about something and could never afford to try it. Maybe you feel stuck at your full-time job that pays the bills and don't really know how to try things out on your own. Or maybe you just got so comfortable with your lifestyle doing something you're good at but don't care for that you were waiting for the right moment to test the waters, and that moment hasn't arrived yet. Wherever you are in life, I'm here to tell you that there is a way to make your dream come true without breaking the bank and causing you anxiety.

So many of my friends and clients, while searching for that deep meaning in their lives and pursuing their passions, have felt tremendous anxiety about starting a new venture. It's a feeling like no other and it begins the moment you say "yes" to yourself and your dream. If you give in to that anxiety, it steers you back to safety and you end up never doing anything with your flower bouquets—or whatever it is you want to do. Some people simply cannot afford to take that chance and try things out, which is why I have been helping people like Amanda with a starting point and a roadmap. Some of them followed my guidance and found their own ways without making financial mistakes they couldn't afford. And some were still too afraid to try but haven't yet given up on their dreams.

As for Amanda, she did a lot of homework and followed my directions. She started slowly and in a familiar territory, and is now running a boutique flower shop, which gave her soul back to her. And every day her flower shop provides her with the confidence she needs to live a happy life without regret.

My passion for numbers and taxes developed in college, and back then I started from zero. I was taking classes full time and, to survive financially, also working as a book-keeper for several small businesses. After the second test in principles of accounting, a brand-new discipline for me, I felt terrible and was certain I had failed it. I thought, "There goes my potential career." When my results were 100 percent I was in shock. "I must be doing something right," I thought, so I kept going. Because I worked as a bookkeeper and learned the foundations at the same time, I was applying accounting concepts and it all made sense to me right away.

Over the years, I applied the concepts I learned to my clients' businesses to help them grow and use financial information for better decision making. Because I was a fast learner, in a few years I developed accounting advisory expertise and started becoming a real problem-solver for my clients, who loved my out-of-the-box approach and ability to speak plain English (as opposed to the language of accounting). It took me about ten years until I realized what business owners were really missing: first, knowing what the must-do steps are *before* they start a business; and second, understanding how to run that business confidently when it comes to money, numbers, and taxes—you know, the stuff that makes so many people cringe. The key is, you've got to nail those back-office fundamentals (money, numbers, and tax matters) as early as you can—it will give you clarity and confidence to secure your dream.

This book is enough for you to start, and start smart. You have all the tools and resources available to you, which will make your journey more enjoyable. If Jeff Bezos could create a giant company from his basement, you can start a business with whatever you've got. All you need is a bold dream and basic knowledge of those back-office fundamentals.

In this book you will find realistic checkpoints to validate, evaluate, and plan your business start. And the best thing is that this material applies to any industry: tech start-ups, service professionals, and product-based businesses.

This book is organized in two parts. Part one covers some of the basic decisions and evaluations you must make before taking your business idea anywhere. After reading this first part you may find that your idea needs further development, is not realistic, is not worth pursuing, is too good to be true. If you do, that is totally *okay*—isn't it a gift to know, before you spend any serious money, that the idea is not worth investing in? But you may also see a way to go forward boldly and succeed.

Part two of the book will give you a framework, a simple step-by-step process you can follow to know the best entity to establish, given your short- and long-term goals; to grasp how to run your business with an understanding of your numbers; to set yourself up for proactively reducing your tax bill; and to know when to ask for help. You will have specific checkpoints and milestones, which will trigger a thought process every time you are ready to launch your next venture. I've also provided you with lists of questions to ask a potential advisor so that you don't have to go it alone.

That's right, this book will hold your hand through the process, and you will get there without going bananas or feeling unworthy, undeserving, and outright foolish. We accountants tend to talk using professional language, assuming you, the client, understand (since it's so basic, ugh). And we often make you feel less intelligent to have even started on this journey. I promise not to do that. Remember: it's not rocket science and you don't need to know *everything* now. You may be inclined to want to free yourself from thinking about this entire topic, but opening up to it and embracing it will actually set you free. By the end of this book you will know exactly how to do what you love and avoid costly mistakes, and you will be empowered to build something special for *yourself.*

PART ONE

DREAM BOLD & SMART

1

Your Dream Awaits

O YOU REMEMBER how you felt when you came up with your cool business idea? Where were you? On the couch? In the shower? Driving your kids to school? If you're like me and most of my clients, you probably wanted to pull over to the side of the road—or step out of the shower—and write down your thoughts immediately. Maybe you called your best friend or your spouse. Maybe you posted your idea on Facebook, so excited for immediate feedback. So thrilled to take the first step on your journey to becoming a business owner.

And then the doubts set in. "What if my brilliant idea isn't so brilliant? What if it's a terrible idea? What if I'm not cut out to pull it off? What if I fail? I want financial freedom, flexibility, family time (or personal interests), and confidence in tomorrow; but what if being my own boss will create the opposite of what I am looking for?"

Do you wish there were a way to bulletproof your business idea? If you say yes, you are not alone. Unless you are a financial professional or an accountant, starting something new and unfamiliar takes a lot of guts and brings with it a lot of anxiety. The further you develop your idea, the more you think about it, and the more you discuss it with your friends and loved ones, the more overwhelmed and anxious you feel, and that nagging thought of "what if it doesn't work?" just keeps popping into your head and doesn't leave you alone.

I hear these concerns almost every day: potential clients walk into my office and say that they are looking for tax or accounting advice, but what I hear they really need is clarity and confidence in their business idea and in managing the back end of a business. Being an aspiring business owner can be scary. You feel like the world needs your idea, that you can quit your job and get more freedom or more time with your kids. But you cannot help thinking: "What if my aunt Susie is right? What if this won't work and I'll lose everything I have? I cannot afford for that to happen! No way!"

Clarity and confidence in your business idea depend on nailing your back-office fundamentals. This means that when you have a good understanding of how to set up financial, accounting, entity structuring, and tax matters right, and when you know how not to lose money on what is not your domain, such as the financial, tax, and accounting matters that come along with a business, you will no longer feel worried, anxious, and scared. It will take a bit of effort to figure out your back office, but you absolutely can do it—you just need a bit of help. And with every chapter of this book you read, you will have more confidence and clarity about what your next step should be.

The truth is that this stuff is also scary, worrisome, and anxiety-causing for existing business owners, not just for aspiring entrepreneurs like you. Lack of clarity and confidence creates that unsettling feeling that eats you up inside. Here is what I mean.

I met Bobby on the plane from California back to New York after an accounting conference I attended. I learned that he was in advertising.

"So, you are a *creative* one," I said. "What's your favorite thing about what you do?"

"Hmm..." Bobby started. "I love helping clients develop their vision, create something unique to them, create partnerships with celebrities and other brands to bring that vision to life. That's the reason I started this business in the first place."

"Interesting! And what do you struggle with most in your business?"

"The financial stuff, you know, and when I talk to my accountant I quickly lose my train of thought and attention, because this stuff is foreign to me—but since I don't want to look like a fool, I just nod as a remedial move to seem that I get it all, and I often don't." Bobby closed his laptop and continued. "To be honest, I never felt confident in any of this, and all that anxiety and worry started when the idea to launch my business first appeared in my head. I could never tell whether I should have an LLC or a corporation, and why to choose one over the other; how do I set up for taxes, how do I know what's deductible, and how should I handle my bookkeeping. None of this was ever clear in my head and it *still* isn't! It's *so* frustrating." Bobby shifted in his seat.

As soon as Bobby said that out loud, I felt shame knowing that, early on, I often did that to clients. I spoke a language they didn't understand and presumed they did, and I didn't provide that much-needed reassurance that they *could* do it, with my help. Reminiscing about those times, I remember how baffled I felt when it came to IT or creative and marketing areas of my business. Now I knew exactly how Bobby, and some of my early clients, felt.

"Yikes!" I thought. "That's a terrible experience, feeling unintelligent, anxious, and not confident enough in your own finances!" Bobby felt this way after being in business for some time, and I can only imagine how he must have felt when he first started out. It must have been nerve-racking and anxiety-causing. And it may have involved a good deal of fear of failing, too—that deep, unsettling fear of "what if" that, no matter how many times we start something new or how long we stay in business, keeps coming back to haunt us.

Many people go to their day jobs and often dislike (or outright hate) what they do. Don't get me wrong; not everyone wants or needs to be an entrepreneur... but I am willing to bet that a great number of you would want to be your own boss, have a flexible schedule, and enjoy a better life balance, if only you knew that you wouldn't fail. You've got a lot at stake taking this huge leap, and if you are reading this book and if you feel this way, you are in the right place. This book will walk you through a process to build a back-office foundation, which is a powerful way to bulletproof your idea and secure your dream. This process will give you confidence and ensure that you will never have to ask yourself if you have what it takes to be an entrepreneur. But before you even get to that, it will also help you assess whether your plan is realistic— and if it's not, what changes you can make so it is.

A favorite movie of mine, *Hidden Figures*, is a true story of three African American women who are math geniuses working at NASA during the Cold War. They perform calculations to build space rockets and calculate trajectories for astronauts' missions. An important scene in the movie unfolds when Katherine Goble, one of the main characters and a numbers genius at the Space Task Group, proposes the use of Euler's method to bring the space capsule back down. This was an unprecedented and risky mission, because the life of John Glenn (the first American to ever orbit the Earth) was at stake. Goble's colleagues deem the suggested method to be "ancient" and are outright skeptical about her idea. But through her calculations, she shows them that it will work. And this is my point: running the numbers is a critical step in any mission—doing it gives you clarity and confidence to move forward.

When you have a business idea that you just can't get out of your head, it may indicate that you would enjoy calling the shots of your own life. It may give you a feeling that, despite your confidence and presumed stability, you were born for something bigger and better. I am not saying that *now* is definitely the right time to launch a business, but I *am* saying that now is the right time to dream bold. Hold on to this feeling and give yourself a chance to build the life you want.

Again, clarity and confidence in your business depend on nailing the financial fundamentals, and that is exactly what we will go over, together and in plain English. Keep one thing in mind: ignoring the possibility of failure won't make you unstoppable, but it will make you ignorant. If you cannot afford to lose money on your idea, then you cannot afford mistakes about money, and this is what we will cover here.

Where Do I Even Begin?

Many questions usually arise when you start validating (in other words, explaining and confirming) your idea with others. And some of these questions are solid concerns: "What's involved?" "How much money do I need to start?" "What help will I need to launch and then to operate?" and "Is there a 'time to market' concern—is the idea likely to be executed by someone else if I take too long?" And, occasionally, "When do I get paid (or get my money back, or both)?"

The next step is the hardest: How will you make money? If you have a platform, whom will you charge—the vendor or the customer or both? How many customers are out there for this service? Is it a limited number? Are they repeat customers or one-timers? If you're selling a product, will you focus on low-cost leadership or high-value differentiation? (Don't worry, we will cover all this. Right now, I just want to plant a seed in your brain.)

Finally, how much do you need in sales to break even every month? How many units of product, service packages, or how much gross revenue do you need to generate to *not borrow to stay in business*? Later in this book you'll see how an outdoor advertising client of mine applied this concept when considering the purchase of a failing print shop, a deal that could have been a complete financial disaster.

I have worked with both successful and struggling businesses. I've seen their owners go through upward and downward cycles, I've advised them when I could, and they listened when they were ready to hear. Some of my clients struggled for years and couldn't stop; some struggled and eventually got their back office under control and built amazing businesses. And it broke my heart to see some people lose a lot of money, money they didn't have, all because they didn't embrace the inevitable: the financial basics.

On a cold Saturday afternoon, Alexis and her husband, Paul, came for an initial consultation. They were sitting in my office, excited, happy, and full of enthusiasm for their business idea. They shared that they had connections in the liquor distribution industry and thought of creating an online platform to bring together liquor stores and distributors for more efficient operations for both sides of the business. Evidently, both of them were passionate about and thrilled with this idea. But I had to be sure that this was more than just passion.

They stumbled when I asked: "How are you going to make money in your business? How will you bring in sales? Which side will be paying for your service?"

Alexis mentioned monthly membership and a few other things I cannot recall, but she could not relate anything specific, such as a plan that would make me optimistic about their chances. That day they left the office still very excited, but I could tell that there was something brewing in their heads.

A few days later I got a call from Alexis. "We decided to open a wine store instead, and we already found a space we are going to rent!"

"Okay," I said. "It's a bit of an investment, initial inventory will probably be your biggest one, but as long as you can afford to get that going and know what you're doing, I will support you in every way I can."

I felt relief that after more careful and realistic consideration, they changed their minds, abandoned their initial idea, and saved themselves probably thousands of dollars in developer fees and a lot of disappointment. You, too, may feel disappointed and discouraged before you even begin your journey, and it's *okay* if you realize that your idea is not a viable one by the end of part one of this book. If that happens to you, if you conclude that your idea as it is will fail, you can still keep going: take the time to develop it and find a way to make it work. It is much better to assess your idea and not launch it because you determine that the math just doesn't work, early on, than to *not* test it out and, as a result, fail and lose money. But it's even better to find a way to make it work and make money!

Back Office Is Not Incidental

Most people don't want to deal with numbers. In fact, numbers are often put on a back burner and left to be done last—also known as *never*. In my experience this approach has never done anyone any good. You can't skip the anxiety-causing number crunching, because it can make or break your business and your personal finances. The only way to grow a successful business, one that can provide for the lifestyle you want, is to acknowledge that you absolutely dislike dealing with the financial stuff, breathe out, and get to it.

Along the way you will come across some of the most common myths related to money and tax matters. You probably believe some or all of them; I've heard them all, and none of them are true. Let's examine a few.

Myth 1: I don't have time for this now. I will deal with it later.

A lot of people believe this. We often think that certain tasks, typically not our domain or specialty, can take the back seat. Back-office stuff (accounting, bookkeeping, taxes, financial management) is usually the culprit. Unfortunately, our passion for what we do can be brutally destroyed by a lack of attention to the seemingly unimportant back office. There are numerous articles and books about different people who won large lottery jackpots and couldn't make it "stick."[1] Check out Sandra Grauschopf's story "Lottery Curse Victims": shockingly, several of them lost everything in short periods of time and their lives were shattered.[2] This says a lot about our natural ability to manage money and gives us an important lesson.

You must pay attention to the "money stuff" at all times. Don't believe the "comforting" thought that it will happen on its own or that someone else will take care of it. Even if you shuffle it all off to an accountant, you must keep a close eye on it. Quite often, my tax practice sees new clients who bring their prior accountants' substandard work and it just breaks my heart. When I point out the errors and missed opportunities, people are usually shocked and disappointed with their previous professional, whom they thought did their job well. And even though, in my heart of hearts, I believe every accountant should provide top-notch service that is error free and uses all the available benefits and opportunities, it is, ultimately, your responsibility to pay attention to the work being done on your behalf. If you don't pay enough attention, it could quickly get out of control.

Myth 2: Everyone has it together.
Or, success just happens for everyone else.
That's a big *lie*! In 2019, the Chrisley family (of the then-famous reality show) were indicted by the Department of Justice for tax-related crimes. It's not uncommon for celebrities to appear in the news, but regular "Joes" and "Janes" run into financial-legal problems, too! My former client's "great tax preparer, because I don't pay much taxes," who was a litigator for the Internal Revenue Service (IRS), several years ago pleaded guilty to aiding in another client's tax evasion.[3]

You might have one of two thoughts as you are reading this: either "Oh my god, it's too much! I won't do it at all, I don't want to go to jail or lose all my money!" or "Stuff like this happens only to the big shots. As long as I stay under the radar, I can do this." I am here to tell you that there is a way to avoid both going to jail for doing something wrong and having that "what if" in your head as you "try to stay under the radar." You can take advantage of all the tax benefits available to you while keeping your peace of mind.

This does not mean you need to do your accounting yourself—that's not at all what I am saying. This book will help you involve the right kind of people. It will give you a process of identifying a great bookkeeper, accountant, and advisor. This will remove the guesswork and the stress while giving you a support system and peace of mind. Boy, does it feel life-changing to work with the best of the best!

Myth 3: I can do this myself— it's simple and I know I can figure it out!

This, by far, is my favorite myth. My practice gets DIYer client requests all the time and, I can tell you, it's always a money maker for me. Why? Because there is always cleanup to do and I can bill prime dollars for it.

See, QuickBooks is the most popular small business book-keeping tool around and is user-friendly. It also gives you the false impression that the financial matters are simple and easy to manage. Please beware! Although I personally stay on top of the technological developments, and my firm is usually an early adopter and tester of every new tech advancement (we research and evaluate every new tool that emerges), I am always conscious that we don't know what we don't know, and that's where it gets dangerous.

Since you may still be tempted to do this on your own, be aware that most small business software makes it easy for you to make a mistake, so much so that I created a masterclass for those who simply cannot afford to pay someone to do their books. I teach my students how, if they must do this them-selves, to do it well and not later spend thousands of dollars paying someone for cleanup. If you do your books right, you will spare yourself from overpaying taxes, and that's valuable, don't you think?

I didn't write this book for you to spend a ton of time dealing with all this "stuff." I wrote it to give you a simple, easy-to-understand, and easy-to-master toolkit that will address most of the issues my firm and I encounter several times a week. Moreover, later in this journey you will learn the signs for when it is time to hire someone to handle the financial aspects and what questions to ask them to be sure their values align with yours.

Myth 4: I don't need to worry about taxes until I'm making money.

That's a good one, don't you think? Unfortunately, it's a lie. A new business typically runs losses—but, if set up and used properly, those losses can provide a great tax benefit for you while you are growing your business.

Remember, when it comes to the IRS, it's all about disclosure and timely filings. They genuinely care about you and want to know all your dealings. I am being sarcastic here, of course (the IRS doesn't care about you much), but what they *do* care about is disclosure and timely filing. So, wherever you are and whatever you do, take care of your business's taxes: file and pay on time. If you have no money left for taxes, you cannot afford your expenses. It's as simple as that.

A few years ago, a new client, Tony, hadn't filed taxes for three years, nor paid them for about four. He was in the middle of a divorce and a custody fight and other personal drama. Personal expenses were flowing through the business account (a *big* no-no, although it is common), too. I saw that there wasn't much room to "cut" expenses, besides his personal rent, which was more than $3,500 per month at the time. But that rent tallied up to $42,000 per year, more than enough for his tax bill. Over the four years that he hadn't paid taxes, his tax bill had snowballed into a whopping $200,000 with interest and penalties.

As much as I tried to help him get out of this rat race, Tony refused to find a more affordable place, which I sort of understand—your home is your home. Here is the thing, though: if you cannot afford your expenses, you'll most likely take shortcuts on your taxes, and, eventually, it's going to come back and bite you. And it's better to know this could happen before it does, so you can avoid anxiety and headaches that can last for years. Don't worry and don't be scared now. The fact that you are reading this already puts you at an advantage, and knowing this ahead of time will give you a tough-love reality check you may need before it's too late.

Your Dream Awaits

Veronica and I have known each other since the first grade and she has always been ambitious, done her own "thing," and not listened to anyone. She has always loved dancing and, during her first year of college, even had her own dance studio.

When she then came to the United States at nineteen, she had to put her dream on hold. She had to survive financially, finish school, and, a bit later, raise a family. Veronica graduated from George Mason University with a marketing degree and got a great job in the marketing department at a large national bank. She enjoyed what she did and became pretty comfortable in that role. She traveled a lot and learned many great marketing strategies, but she couldn't shake off the feeling that something was missing in her life. She couldn't yet put her finger on it, but she knew that a great job with a regular salary, good benefits, and an enviable career trajectory just wasn't cutting it for her. She secretly hoped to one day be laid off so that she could work for herself and run her own life.

One Tuesday afternoon she and all her bank colleagues gathered together at their headquarters for the CEO's address. She sat next to her team members and they seemed to be having a great time, excitement all around. In his speech, the CEO shared the bank's many accomplishments and his vision for the company's future. He also shared that he had long had a dream of the bank growing to become what it now was: a strong and highly profitable financial organization. He then thanked all of the employees for helping him build this vision of his and he was excited for the future.

Veronica stopped breathing for one quick moment. "Wait a second," she thought. "I should have been building *my* dream instead!"

That moment was Veronica's turning point. She decided to quit. After a brief conversation with her husband, her plan was confirmed. She gave notice at her job, and it was the happiest day of her life.

As Veronica told me about it, sounding all excited on the phone, I had a moment of déjà vu. I suddenly recalled my own journey a few years before that, when I worked for an accounting firm. I had enjoyed the steady pay and the hands-on tax experience, but I always knew that I wanted to work for myself and call my own shots. In fact, the first week I left my full-time job, it felt incredibly liberating to not have to go to work on a weekday. I can remember that feeling to this day.

That being said, I am a more pragmatic type, and certainly not all of us can afford to quit our jobs first and then immediately start doing what we love. Veronica was fortunate that her family could afford for her to start right away, but most of us, myself included, have to build our boldest dreams slowly while working full time and sometimes pulling all-nighters. That's what I'd done for two years, and I remember my bosses and colleagues being clueless about why I was so tired all the time at work. I just couldn't let them in on my big secret: that after I left the office, I went home and worked toward *my* dream.

You may think that I got lucky or that I am special, but I am not. I knew deep in my heart that I did not want to work the way our industry tells us we have to work to make a decent living. So, I took the time to understand what I did and did not want in life and I built up my client base slowly until I could leave my full-time job without creating a financial meltdown for myself.

As for Veronica, she stayed true to herself, and over the past five years, she has been building her dream, one brick at a time, while also caring for her family. She now owns her own dance studio in Virginia, and I often watch her Instagram stories, which constantly emit a lot of fiery energy—more than enough to go around.

So, pause for a moment, close your eyes and picture your boldest dream. What does it look like? What will it take to make it a reality? What or who can jeopardize your dream and prevent it from happening? Note these attributes, add today's date to the page, and save it, kind of like a time capsule, so that you can go back to it in a few years and be proud of how far you've come. It will be amazing and I am willing to bet on that.

Know that you are not alone and, I promise, it's absolutely doable. At the end of this book, you will have the tools and a roadmap to launch *any* business idea. You will have confidence and will know and understand your numbers. Confidence in your back office will provide clarity about what needs to be done to make your idea happen. You may even someday switch roles with your accountant, and, instead of them advising and reassuring you, or worse, intimidating you with big words and fancy scenarios, *you* will be in charge: you will tell them, "I got this," and know exactly what to do. Wouldn't that feel great and liberating?

Today is the day for *you* to act and be true to yourself. Starting is the scariest part, and you may even have doubts and limit yourself with your own fears. You may not be able to shake off a feeling of unworthiness. And I want you to challenge yourself and say, "Why not me?" Who's to say that *your* dream won't make a difference in the world? Who's to say that *your* dream won't make the lives of other people better? Your time is *now*, and your dream awaits.

First, though, you will need to ask yourself some important questions and make a few critical decisions. And if you've already started a business, you will have an opportunity to guarantee that you're doing it right. So, let's dive in.

2

Is Your Idea Any Good?

DO YOU THINK your idea is the next Facebook? Or maybe the next iPhone? What about your idea excites you and gives you a "this is it!" feeling? If you're anything like Lenny, a client of mine, you get excited and start planning business empires that *could* be built. Lenny is an entrepreneur at heart and loves starting new things, finding new ventures and ways to make money by filling a void—and I often have to bring him back down to Earth.

Getting carried away by a business idea is easy. Many start-ups never make it to the market, and of those that do, many never make it over a five-year hurdle, for several reasons: cash mismanagement, ego-driven decisions, and lack of planning, just to name a few. As an "almost-preneur," in this book you will find a roadmap, a plan to make sure that you don't waste a ton of money and energy developing an idea just to find out that it's not worth much.

We will begin by imagining your end goal, your bigger dream. I offer you real-life examples from my practice, which should help you develop your idea. In this chapter we will cover the necessary calibration of your business idea. We will test your assumptions and understand your limitations and must-haves. One thing to keep in mind, though, is that although you should be clear on what you are planning to do, you should be ready to correct your course if another route presents itself and makes more sense.

If you're already in business, use this chapter to get laser-focused on what your business is about and your end goal.

Rick Sold His Business for Millions and Started Another

Rick was a true entrepreneur. In his early sixties, he happened to be my mentor-volunteer while I went for my graduate degree. I immediately connected with him. He was an energetic and successful business owner, aka serial entrepreneur, who, just before internet shopping overhauled catalog shopping, sold his business and started another one.

Before calling it quits one day and starting his first catalog shopping business out of his basement, Rick was a successful telecom sales executive at a large company. He was superb at what he did, but family, flexibility, and freedom (the benefits often associated with entrepreneurship) were ultimately more important to him. So, he started out on his own.

Rick was determined to succeed as an entrepreneur no matter what. He sold graphic hardware and software, business to business, using print catalogs that he shipped to companies so that they could place their orders. Rick operated at a very low margin, and he soon realized that his true business was *not* selling hardware or software: it was selling ad space to vendors willing to pay big bucks for prime placements in his catalogs. So, he started approaching companies and offering them higher-priced ad space. This completely changed the direction of Rick's business.

A couple of years later he realized that online shopping was about to replace print catalogs, and he saw a better opportunity in licensing original illustration and photography to the same markets that he had served via his catalogs. So, he transformed his catalog company into an online aggregator of imagery. He made deals with other image producers for rights to their works, and then sold licensing rights to graphic design firms, advertising agencies, and companies seeking to incorporate photography into their advertisements or other media. The cool thing about selling images is that all the inventory is virtual: all you have to do is create a digital infrastructure to search and download pictures. It was expensive and not-so-easy but it succeeded. In 1998, he sold this business for more than $10 million to a larger company in the same space and happily retired, able to live the life he wanted.

Frank's Idea Evolved into a Multimillion-Dollar Venture

I met energetic twenty-three-year-old Frank as I did the monthly books for my then-client Michael. Frank was the new executive assistant and I immediately loved his attitude of "whatever needs to be done to get us where we need to go, I am doing it *now*" because it connected with my own personal approach to everything I have done in life. Frank worked for Michael for about two years and fell in love with fashion. In 2011, he left Michael's firm and launched his own company, which has evolved and grown tremendously over time and prompted him to grow with it.

At a young age, Frank turned out to be a true entrepreneur: he identified what was missing in the fashion industry and developed a concept to fill the void. Frank and his partner, Matt, developed an algorithm that would connect new-generation fashion designers who created affordable "celebrity-look" garments to regular people, so that they could "shop the celebrity look" on a budget.

Throughout 2012, Frank worked on developing his company's revenue streams—ways to monetize his idea. In the same year he pitched it to a prominent Boston-based law firm that, at the time, had a special legal assistance program for start-ups. The firm would provide up to $80,000 in legal services, including patent filings, if they "believed" in your idea. So, Frank was motivated and fine-tuned his value proposition.

I remember meeting Frank for lunch one day in the city, and as he described how his idea was evolving to a new level, he said, "It's not *if* I will be successful, it's *when*." I got goosebumps when he said that, and I saw something in his eyes that I will remember for a long time. It was the look of a passionate person who would do whatever it takes, who would bend over backward to make his dream happen.

Over the years Frank's initial idea and passion have changed significantly. In fact, there is nothing left of his 2011 plan besides the company name. Frank paid attention to trends and developments within the fashion industry but also in technology. His company, D'Marie, is now the industry leader in monetizing the value of social media. Frank's patented engine puts a dollar value on every social media post by a celebrity or an influencer. This tool gives various companies across several industries an ability to show the value of their models, talents, and influencers to the hiring brand. Here is why it works.

In New York City, every time a fashion brand hires a model for a lookbook or a collection photoshoot, the agency can give the hiring brand the value of that model wearing its clothes in the model's Instagram post, so that the brand gets even more exposure to more people. This is something that modeling agencies were never able to do before, and it adds tremendous value for them. This is just one example of how D'Marie's technology is used today.

My dear Frank went beyond that and took his company to an even higher level. He now uses the technology D'Marie developed to do brand makeovers using influencer networks and their value. Frank can fairly easily put a dollar value on a celebrity endorsement of a brand based on that celebrity's social media status and ranking. Over a decade, D'Marie has evolved into an amazing company, and I am holding my breath to see what the future holds for Frank. I am also very honored to be a part of his success.

A CPA's Lack of Technological Adaptation Nearly Sank Him

A few years ago, I freelanced for another accountant, Leslie, to make some extra cash. It was just him, an assistant, and a freelancer like me. He had a pretty interesting tax practice but was *old school,* which is fairly common for accountants.

Leslie had computer-based tax preparation software and piles of paper documents. Every time one of his three-hundred-plus clients was buying a house or refinancing and needed a copy of some form, he needed to find the files, scan them, and send them. Leslie's document system depended heavily on physical paper. Also, in this age of paperless every-thing, he still sent out a paper tax return to every client and agonized over reorganizing a printed copy himself in the order of his liking.

During the three years that I freelanced for Leslie, I noticed how hard he worked and how stressed he always was. Then I realized that he preferred stress over a better sys-tem. Even though many accountants have long switched to paperless, partially or fully, Leslie was holding on as long as he could. I, on the other hand, always adopt new technology and new ways of doing things, even though, like many people, I don't *love* change. I eventually left because Leslie's approach didn't work well for my brain.

During the 2020 pandemic, which happened in the middle of tax season, Leslie was in a real pickle. Because of a weak immune system, he could not risk having other people in the office, yet he did not allow paper files to be taken out of the office. Because he had failed to adapt to a new (and better) way of running the business, he had a nervous breakdown in March that year and couldn't function for days, and his tax season stretched out like a top-brand garbage bag.

Leslie's story isn't unique: even large companies often fail to recognize a trend and adapt. You and I can both learn from others' mistakes so we won't need to make them ourselves. All we must do is follow trends and look into the future.

It's Your Turn to Make History

Now it's your turn to make history, even if, for now, it's your family's history. Devote some time to thinking about and evaluating your business idea. You do not need to spend weeks or months planning: be cognizant of your timing to market. Ask yourself these questions, note your answers, and create your time capsule today.

Question 1: Do you have passion for this business idea? Why?

Did your idea come out of a pain you've been dealing with for years? Maybe it grew out of your life story? Or is it something you always wanted to do? Do you think you "discovered" yourself at this point in your life? What I mean is: do you know what will make you happy and let you look back on your path and say, "I have no regrets"? Now put your idea to the test: will it bring you closer to your "best life"?

Question 2: What do you offer? A product or a service?

Remember Rick's story of having a catalog sales business and turning it into an ad space business? Think about what you are selling, what problem you are solving for your customers. What will their lives look like after they engage your company? Will it be better? How? Keep in mind that every business is, realistically, a product business. If you offer a service or a solution, you *can* package it and create levels of your offering. With a clear offer it's a lot easier to sell it later.

Question 3: Who is your ideal customer? Do you have several customer avatars?

Can you relate to your customer? Maybe you've struggled with the same problem before? Maybe your customer is an earlier version of you? Can your product or service make their lives easier? At what stages of life are they now? Where do they want to be?

Question 4: What's your value proposition? Who is your competition and what makes you better?

What solution are you offering to your customers? Why is it important to them? Is it a valuable product or service? And how much would *you* be willing to pay for it?

Question 5: How will you make money?

Many of my existing and potential clients with start-ups never drill down in their revenue-generating activities—in other words, how exactly they will make money. Consider the following questions (in chapter 8, you will get in-depth guidance on these): Will you sell volume and make a small margin? Or will you sell a "prestige" product and make a high margin? How many potential customers are out there? Who else is fighting for them? Can you run out of customers? Will your product or service be a one-time or repeat purchase?

A good example of this, although not a product-based business, is attorneys who do wills and estate planning. Networking is tough for them because their clients are often one-time clients. They prepare a will, update it maybe once or twice, create or update a few trusts, and that is it, they're back in the hunter's seat. For traditional accounting firms, as a counterexample, the situation is a bit different. A new client most likely will stay year after year and bring repeat income, which makes it predictable, more or less. What is it like for your business idea?

Question 6: Will you have one main revenue stream or several?

I want to ask you to write down your answer to this question, as it's an important one. (As a matter of fact, write down your answers to all the questions in this chapter. It will help you in your future endeavors.) In part two of this book we will talk about your business idea launch and your choice of entity. Oftentimes having several distinct revenue streams can make for better-than-usual tax planning. For absolutely separate business lines (or departments), you may need an additional entity not only for business separation but also for tax reduction purposes. So, get creative.

Question 7: What is your personal goal for this business?

Do you see yourself running this business forever? Do you want to sell it later to a willing buyer for a fair price? What do you want this business to provide for *you* and *your family*?

You may simply want it to pay bills, or it can provide a good lifestyle and flexibility—it can also help you retire early. What would make *you* happy?

Remember, "a lot of money" is not a goal in and of itself. Once you have that, what will make you happy (refer to question 1)? Be bold and be honest with yourself. If your goals seem outrageously brave, that's okay, and if your goal changes and evolves, that's okay, too. Remember Frank? Nothing is left of his initial business idea to be a platform for aspiring fashion designers, and that's totally fine.

Question 8: What is your "space domination" goal?

Remember the Space Task Group in the *Hidden Figures* movie (based on NASA's real Space Task Group)? The ultimate goal was *not* to launch a rocket into Earth's orbit. That was only an intermediate goal. The entire country was in the "fight of our lives" (as Al Harrison, the head of Space Task Group at Langley Research Center, told his team, referring to the Cold War), and the fight was to dominate space. Successfully launching John Glenn's Friendship 7 into orbit in 1962 was a stepping-stone for the United States of America to then launch a manned mission to the moon in 1969.

Why does this matter to you? It matters because you need to go deeper and understand whether your business idea is the equivalent of John Glenn's mission or whether it is a bigger, more important idea of "space domination." You may not know right away, and moreover, the idea can evolve and change, and that is perfectly normal. You may also have several possibilities for your idea's future. I encourage—even urge—you to explore them and save your thoughts for a periodic checkup and evaluation. In other words, keep it close.

Having a vision and a long-term goal and an understanding of the motivation behind your idea as it is today can help you make critical decisions about it in the future. It is also what will set you apart from everyone else who may have a similar idea. And you wouldn't believe how many folks aren't doing it, so you are way ahead of the game.

In my practice, I don't only come across success stories—I have plenty of unsuccessful launches to share later in the book, like Anthony, who got carried away by an idea and investor money; or another client, who refused to get a cheaper office space, was living off past successes, and went broke. I've seen plenty of that. My own business, up until not long ago, was a great example of not developing the "big-picture" goal. Since I was kids-focused while my two children were babies (for each of their first three years), I never treated my accounting practice as a business. It was a passion that paid my bills. Because of that, it was so much harder to develop it—to get new, established clients and realize the value I could deliver to them. Only when my firm ranked in the top-fifteen in a global contest amongst accounting firms did I realize that I've got so much good to share. I am telling you this now to let you know that your story is unlike everyone else's, that your voice is unique, and that there are people who need your solution and will buy from you *because* of your story and your voice.

The Muse

As an author, I do believe in the muse. I am confident that we are not all born geniuses with unique ideas, that we are merely conductors of those ideas—messengers, if you will. We all come to this planet with a mission, and sometimes that mission is to follow a calling, an opportunity that's knocking on our door.

If you don't answer, it can find someone else's door to knock on, but then you have effectively not answered your calling. Now, you may or may not believe in it, and it is certainly your choice, but my goal is for you to answer your calling with some basic tools. So, do you know what you're all about now? What you want and how you are going to get there? Do you know your endgame?

Stop here and look over all the answers you have written down. Do they give you a clear sense of direction? Do your notes give you "butterflies" from excitement or does your stomach hurt just thinking about it? Are you certain that your offer is clearly needed? Remember, this is *your* ship of dreams. And now is the time to find out what could sink it and what will keep it sailing.

3

Do You Know
Your Risks?

I N 1628 THERE was a ship that was just as ambitious as the
"unsinkable" *Titanic* of the twentieth century. The *Vasa*,
a Swedish navy warship, sank within twenty minutes
of setting sail, to the horror of the public watching from the
shore.[1] It turned out that the ship was too top-heavy; when
it met a strong gust of wind from the side, it tilted too far,
quickly took on water and foundered, despite everyone being
sure it was a one-of-a-kind ship.

Just over a century later in Britain, John Wilkinson, a
prominent iron-obsessed entrepreneur, created and launched
a barge made of cast iron.[2] Everyone around him was skeptical that something so heavy would be able to float. Not only
did it *not* sink, it surprised everyone with its ability to transport heavy loads, and it revolutionized river transport forever.

How do you stack up against risks? Do you know your
own "sink" and "sail" factors? Have you thought about what
will keep you afloat? In this chapter you will do a simple risk
assessment and a more complex SWOT analysis. The latter
framework is typically taught in MBA programs and is widely

used in business, including businesses that have been around for years. The former is a tool that allows you dissect and analyze risks, to which your business idea is susceptible. Let's look at SWOT first.

SWOT stands for "strengths," "weaknesses," "opportunities," and "threats," where strengths and weaknesses refer to internal characteristics, and opportunities and threats refer to external forces. Divide a piece of paper into four squares, one for each of the SWOT elements. It should look something like this:

Strengths (Internal)	Weaknesses (Internal)
Opportunities (External)	Threats (External)

First, let's focus on your strengths. That's the easy part, as they are typically where you would start and from where your idea originates. What do you offer that's different from other businesses? How can you improve your clients' lives with your product or service? What value do you deliver to your customer? Value, in particular, will be crucial in chapter 8, when we talk about setting the "just right" price for your product or service, so pay close attention to what you note here. Your strengths will be your value building blocks, and you'd better know them really well.

The next square will show your business's weaknesses. Knowing your internal limitations will propel you to address them up front and to find ways to turn them into strengths. Going "all out" with weaknesses may feel overwhelming at first and may even make you feel stuck and/or depressed for a moment, but know that these feelings are absolutely expected and will eventually pass, so just don't pay too much attention to them right now. You are doing this exercise for you, and nobody else needs to see it. It takes a strong person to think and talk about their weaknesses, and my advice is to keep going.

The opportunities square will help you focus on and strengthen your value proposition. Oftentimes our idea (aka "strength") emerges because there is an external need in our environment and our proposition will fill some kind of void. Understanding and analyzing the opportunities is important, as is brainstorming about how you can take advantage of your environment to launch your business idea to market with great timing.

Threats take our attention to the external forces influencing our business, and, boy, can they make us weak at the knees. This square, by far, will produce the most anxiety. But every business has threats, just like every job does. Being aware of their existence and understanding them is half the battle, because our brain is wired to look for ways to overcome and protect against threats. But for your brain to do that effectively, you need to be realistic about what those threats are.

SWOT Case Study

The best way to understand any concept is by looking at examples, so here is an example of a SWOT analysis of my accounting advisory firm. Now, I do need to mention that going "naked" and exposing my firm's SWOT is a new adventure for me, but I believe in acknowledging my weak spots so that I can become stronger, and so should you.

Let's start with the strengths.

My firm has developed several service-level packages, typically tailored to every client, because all entrepreneurs have individual needs. When a client follows my firm's advice, they get where they want to be financially. Over the years we have perfected our system of providing not only business guidance but also empathy and mental support, because it's not an easy journey to be on and can feel a bit lonely at times. Our top clients no longer get frightened by the numbers; they use them to make timely and smart business decisions.

What makes my firm special is the toolbox of services we offer and the ability to bring all the tools to each client. Here is what I mean: besides doing the traditional tax work—filing your taxes and closing the books—we offer price psychology advice, outside controller service, and a proactive tax-lowering strategy. For the client this means that when we talk about cash flow forecast and raising prices, we keep taxes in mind, too. My firm is not completely unique in this—there are other firms that offer similar services—but the combination of all our tools provides clients with support where they need it most, all in one place.

Take a look at weaknesses.

Now remember, weaknesses are internal limitations. My firm is still very small and I don't necessarily want it to get big. With "getting big" usually comes conveyor-belt-style work and I really enjoy a deeper, more personal relationship with clients.

For a CPA firm, size can be a huge limitation, because many tasks still depend on my involvement and largely depend on me. Also, because of our fairly small size, we cannot take on large corporate projects, such as consolidated conglomerates, which usually require a large staff. The important thing, when it comes to a weakness, is to try to turn it into a strength, so I have worked with a coach to develop procedures so that the office runs like clockwork, and now I am training bookkeepers and accountants to hire.

The bottom line is that I am aware of my firm's limitations. I focus on helping smaller companies survive and thrive, with a personal and dedicated approach, instead of chasing larger, higher-revenue projects I cannot handle and trying to be everything to everyone.

Understand your opportunities.

A great opportunity for my firm is the changing landscape of accounting service offerings. Influential accountants such as Ron Baker, Mark Wickersham, and Dominique Molina are helping accountants like me provide a different level of service to a smaller number of clients and have a good quality of life while following our passion for numbers.

Value billing and ditching an hourly rate is the inevitable future of CPA firms and is already my firm's present. Why? Think about a typical accountant. It's nearly impossible to devote a set number of hours each week to every client if you have three hundred of them. Yet it's hard to earn a good living when you have fewer clients. And how could I possibly incorporate all my experience, knowledge, and constant self-education into an hourly rate?

In 2018, my firm went from hourly to value billing, which means that I no longer track hours spent on a client. Prior to that, I noticed that clients, with the billing rate on their minds, would often withhold questions and make financial moves without asking us first. In some cases this had significant monetary consequences. Here is a good example.

Many years ago, a client couple were buying their first home. They heard that if they took the funds out of their retirement (up to $10,000), they would not pay any tax. So, they didn't ask me, and when tax time came and the year was over, they got an unpleasant surprise. It turned out that they had taken the funds out of their respective employer-sponsored pension plans, rather than from an IRA, which is a retirement account you would set up on your own at the bank. So not only was their withdrawal taxable (it is taxable in either case) but they were assessed a 10 percent penalty in addition to the income tax, which could have been avoided if they had first rolled the funds into an IRA. A $2,000 mistake on a $20,000 withdrawal.

With value billing, my firm has a much smaller number of clients, and service packages include questions throughout the year, meetings, ongoing support, and planning. Yes, it's a more expensive service, but it serves both the client and the firm. The client now doesn't have to guess whether their decisions are best from the tax and business management perspective—they know for a fact because they can consult with their accountant. The accountant can devote more time to clients who need it most and have a transformational impact on their businesses and lives.

Finally, know the threats.

Every business has threats—they're inevitable. Every industry is prone to changes, technological innovations, and competition. It's all about how you handle your internal progress and evolve.

You may have already guessed that for an accounting firm, a big threat is artificial intelligence. With lightning-fast developments in "smart" technologies, which can mimic our brain functions, no industry will be unaffected by AI. In our services, machines will do data entry and bookkeeping, post information into the tax program, and make some assumptions. This will eventually lead to a lot of tasks currently assigned to staff not being needed at all.

My firm has been studying new approaches to accounting advisory, looking at new ways to provide value, and developing a firm of the future for several years now, so we continuously work to evolve. I often meet with former colleagues of mine and I am amazed at how many folks are still in denial of progress and think that they can get away with the "same old" approach. Well, I can see that there is already a surge of new-generation accountants, so I can safely bet on traditional firms missing out on new opportunities.

Here is what my simple SWOT looks like:

Strengths (Internal)	Weaknesses (Internal)
Several powerful tools for small business owners in my toolbox	Small firm, unable to take on huge projects
Opportunities (External)	**Threats (External)**
Industry (and firm) shift to value billing	Artificial intelligence
Fewer clients, more involved service	Competition

SWOT for a Business Idea

It may seem easy to dissect an existing business, but doing this exercise when you're really excited about a new venture is a bit more difficult. A business idea is harder to analyze because there are many unknowns and many assumptions are necessary. To make matters worse, our ego often comes into play and we listen to it, sometimes blindly.

When Olga was about twenty-one she met a wonderful young man named Sergey, and after a short while they started living together (and eventually got married). They both had Russian roots and really enjoyed Russian-style food. One evening Olga and Sergey were sitting in the kitchen and had an idea: "Maybe we should open our own Russian grocery store in our town." Truth be told, it was a big town, with no similar stores in the area.

Sergey was a project manager by trade and this idea was a "challenge accepted" project, so he jumped at it but, being a project manager, he suggested "running the rough numbers" first, which they agreed to do together. They pulled out a piece of paper and started writing down costs.

The idea was to get to the break-even number: the amount of daily or weekly revenue needed to not have to borrow money to operate. They started with fixed costs, costs that they would have to pay anyway, like rent, utilities, and staff. They decided to start with possibly one part-time person, so that both of them could have a day off. They narrowed it down to a monthly number of $30,000. They would also have to invest in the initial purchase of stock products and equipment (fridges and shelves—used ones, for now), which was about $20,000.

They agreed that they would be selling Russian-style products such as cold cuts, kefir, meat ravioli (pelmeni), farmer's cheese, chocolates, teas, coffees, dried fruits and nuts, cakes, and yogurts, and that they would serve cooked food buffet-style. Naturally, they would have some variable costs—costs of products sold with a markup. Those would depend on a few factors, like keeping a certain quantity in stock (which means investing in stock up front) and monthly turnover (products purchased monthly) but, basically, the costs monthly would range from $30,000 to $35,000. Another thing to keep in mind is that certain products have a very short shelf life and need to be checked for expiry and discarded. This can mean throwing out a lot of product or selling expired products by accident, both of which can be costly.

Initially, Olga and Sergey were excited about their idea: it was fun and *cool*. Their egos were showing them this picture of success and entrepreneurship and flexibility and rainbows. Once they did a simple numbers analysis, they quickly realized that to break even, they would need a daily revenue of about $1,000. It was a realistic and down-to-earth estimate and it was a big number to get consistently. Truth be told, there were not enough people in the area who would come to the store every few days for the couple to sustain this level of daily revenue. Sergey and Olga quickly realized it was too big a daily target and abandoned the idea for good. Phew! You can see what their swot would look like on the next page.

One can only imagine where this couple would have been today if they had invested a ton of money into this idea and had to shut down in a few months, with no jobs (they would have had to leave their jobs to operate at a minimum cost) and no business. What a disaster has been avoided! At the same time, the opportunity of a growing Russian community as well as no similar stores in the area is a pretty strong argument to revisit this idea in a few years. Thankfully, you have this book to prevent you from going down a path leading to a financial disaster, so take the time to assess your swot and plan ahead.

Strengths (Internal)	Weaknesses (Internal)
Strong business management skills	No specific retail experience
Opportunities (External)	**Threats (External)**
No similar store in the area A growing Russian community	Not enough people-traffic to be able to break even

Assess Your Risks

Let's take a closer look at the weaknesses and threats one more time, and this time set up a simple two-by-four table (get a downloadable sample at dreamboldbook.com), which you will review as needed, or as you feel things change and evolve. The columns will denote what you can control and what you cannot control and the rows will rate the likelihood of a weakness or threat event occurring. Assign a likelihood factor to every threat or weakness you identify, on a probability scale from one to one hundred, along with a dollar value for each risk.

As with a SWOT analysis, you will come up with risks that your business is susceptible to. A good place to start is with the weaknesses and threats from the previous section. What would it cost you if each of these risks happened? Or, how much would you forgo in revenue if they were to happen?

	Can Control	**Cannot Control**
Chance of happening: 75–100		
Chance of happening: 50–74		
Chance of happening: 25–49		
Chance of happening: 1–24		

Evaluate them one at a time and assign a dollar-amount range based on best-case to worst-case scenarios. Going through this exercise will provide you with several important tools. It will give you with a risk spectrum, so that you know what could go wrong and what your exposure is.

Let's take my firm as an example. The weakness is that my firm is small and unable to take on huge (and potentially highly profitable) projects. Next, let's look at a few threats. Artificial intelligence is one; another is that if my clients experience a significant economic downturn it could adversely affect their ability to pay. Artificial intelligence will eventually be able to take over data entry for tax returns, but my firm will replace preparation-only work with clients we advise, so, even though I assigned a dollar value to the AI threat, I have a plan to make up for it when it happens—which you should also have for each type of risk. There are other risks I can control, like being the only senior accountant in the firm. However, I am aware of and comfortable with those risks. I delegate certain tasks already, but need to delegate more, so in my quarterly strategy sessions I often review what additional tasks I can give to my team to handle to reduce that risk. Take a look at what my form would look like, and keep in mind that the dollar values are estimates of income lost and there may be risks I am not aware of, too.

	Can Control	**Cannot Control**
Chance of happening: 75–100	Unaware of any	AI; risk: $40,000
Chance of happening: 50–74	Small firm, inability to take large projects; risk: $100,000	Economic downturn; risk: $80,000
Chance of happening: 25–49	Unaware of any	Unaware of any
Chance of happening: 1–24	All work done by me; risk: $200,000	Unaware of any

You will notice the item "all work done by me." I could potentially control that risk and remove the chance of the business shutting down if I were unable to work. But I would need to hire someone with tax and accounting knowledge and skills, which would demand a significant cash outflow in the form of a salary, related taxes, and benefits. So, even though it's a controllable risk in theory, there is a significant cost to control it. A possible solution could be to secure a buy-sell agreement with another professional to take over in the unlikely event of me being unable to take care of the business. A setup like this is an effective plan to address that risk at a pretty low cost.

Do this homework for your risks to understand if you can reduce both the likelihood and the dollar exposure ahead of time or find a way to leverage it. Whether it is an "emergency" plan or a course correction, be sure to know your "worst-case scenarios" for the financial exposure. For the "can control" boxes with higher likelihoods of occurrence—the two upper-left boxes—prepare a plan of action, a reasonable and an adequate one. For the two lower boxes in both columns, I suggest that you keep them in the back of your mind and review them periodically. Awareness alone will help you react deliberately if a sudden situation, like a recession or a pandemic, occurs. Print a visual and put it up somewhere you can see it daily. Make it available for your team or your "board" (more on this later), so that they can think about it, too.

Filling in this table will produce some short-term anxiety for sure. You will doubt yourself, wondering why you even started this whole ordeal and wanting to quit. As you feel that gut-wrenching anxiety, remember that our brains are wired for success, so when we present a problem, our brains look for a solution, subconsciously. If you trust and believe in yourself, your anxiety will soon transform into a strategy and action-able steps, which will bring peace and clarity to you.

Now that you've sat down and at least outlined a few of your risks and honestly assessed your SWOT, you are ahead of many business owners and are better prepared to pivot your business if a risk becomes a reality. Knowing your risks now, you will develop a strategy and a plan of attack.

Now the question is, who is going to help you with that attack?

4

Who Is on Your Team of "Geniuses"?

SEVERAL YEARS AGO, I experienced a mindset shift and my business transformed. I happened to read a book that made me realize that if I continued being a solo accountant, which is what I wanted for many years, I would never be free. It dawned on me that I would never get to the point in my business and life that initially drove me out on my own! I knew I needed to change something, so I joined a coaching program. During one of the sessions, our coaching group had to look at all the possible functions of an accounting firm and note the hats we wore in our accounting businesses. The second phase of the exercise entailed identifying the "hats" we would want to eventually delegate, as well as the "hats" we wanted to keep doing. I realized that I genuinely disliked many of the daily tasks I did for my firm. So, I only selected about three to four tasks I would love to keep doing "forever" and decided that I would focus on eventually delegating the rest. It also became apparent that what I really enjoyed doing was the crème de la crème of my work, the most impactful and life-changing activities for clients.

Maybe you have long had a passion for something, but I will let you in on a little secret: when people start a business, it almost always begins with a passion, but as they get into the grind of it, they are often forced to deal with everything in order to keep going. And I mean *everything*. They wear many hats but only love the one part that inspired them to start. Please honor and remember this as you go.

You may be thinking, "It's just me, sitting in a little nook in my home, daydreaming. Why do I have to imagine a whole company I may or may not have years down the road? What if I want to just remain a one-person shop?" And I get it: it seems like this proposition is too far-fetched and promises to bore you to death. Well, humor me, will you?

Remember *Hidden Figures* and your goal of space domination? How did developing and building up that goal make you feel? Did you get goosebumps on your skin just thinking about it? Maybe you haven't figured it out yet and are still searching. Maybe you abandoned that business idea altogether. Or maybe you felt that you were finally starting something you were born to do. If you're not feeling ready, it may make sense for you to set this section aside for a little bit. But if you're feeling like you're beginning your life's true mission, this step will help you make smooth transitions as you grow and find the right people. And if you're somewhere in the middle or are already running a business, stay with me.

Your Org Chart

Review the structure on the next page. It will not only become critical later, as you hire the right people for well-defined roles, but it will also provide you with a roadmap *today*, which will help you further develop and grow your business idea.

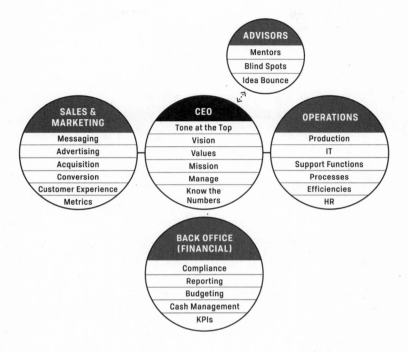

Sketch out an organizational chart that represents the way you see your company three years from today. Develop the roles you will need and determine which hats you want to keep wearing in your business and which you will want to delegate. This process doesn't have to take a lot of time, can be totally ambitious, and doesn't need to be overly complicated, but doing it will help you realize your vision with the least number of your own mistakes.

With this clarity, you will plant a seed in your mind now that you will come back to as soon as you need to. When you are ready to hire, and when you are experiencing rapid growth, you will know exactly what type of person you need for each role in your business.

Take a look at an organizational chart that reflects the way I encourage you to structure your business. This chart will help you think ahead and understand early on which "hats" you want to wear—what part of the process you enjoy and see yourself doing for a long time. Thinking about it now will focus your efforts and make them precise.

It begins with you, the CEO, the tone you set at the top, and your vision and values. Set those early on. What is non-negotiable for you? What are you not willing to sacrifice, ever? Then think about your mission and how you want your company to be perceived. You will need to manage the three functions of a business—sales and marketing, back office, and operations—to gather critical information so that you can make knowledgeable and strategic decisions.

Sales and marketing is an important function, and it is three-fold. First, your messaging and advertising will enable you to appear in front of customers' eyes, so that they learn more about you. That's your customer acquisition process. Second, you will need to develop your sales process and focus on customer lead conversion. Third is your customers' experience and the service you provide. Establishing metrics to manage all these processes and measure their effectiveness is critical, so come up with ways to track your progress in all three areas.

The focus of this book is the *back office*, which centers on developing your compliance, bookkeeping, and budgeting systems and managing your key performance indicators (KPIs). KPIs give you your business dashboard at your fingertips, and the goal of your dashboard is to provide financial data for all your business decisions. Cash flow management is the most critical part of this business function, and I suggest you keep a tight grip on it for a while.

Finally, *operations* includes all the support functions of your business, such as production of the product or service you're selling, all computer systems and processes, automations, creating and supporting the entire business's processes and efficiencies, and ensuring your employees are taken care of through HR procedures.

And then you'll notice the stand-alone block: *advisors*. That is a satellite function. It's your team of advisors, people who have agreed to support you, who mentor you and point out your blind spots. Choose people whose opinions you value. They will help you figure out what you don't know and act as sounding boards as you flesh out your ideas.

Early on you will perform most of these roles and wear those hats, and that is perfectly okay: it will save you a lot of money and you will get firsthand experience in managing all these roles. Later, as you hire other people to perform some of the functions, you will know exactly where they fit in and what kind of person you need to take on that role and rock it.

As a result of wearing all those hats, you will be able to set expectations and minimum performance standards and pay attention not just to initial impressions and résumés but to the ability of a prospective employee to excel at a particular job. Make a note—this will be critical later.

A Board of Advisors

"Board of advisors" sounds a bit big and intimidating and possibly even expensive, but it doesn't have to be. In fact, this is probably one of the best things you can do for yourself and it doesn't have to cost a fortune—or anything, for that matter. The most important takeaway here is that it's often hard to start or run a business alone but so many do it, out of fear of their idea being stolen, or out of confidence that they *don't need help*. Consider this example.

David runs a menswear brand called Nasty Pig, a leader in the world of LGBTQ fashion and one of the best-run companies I have ever worked with, and here is why. David never went to business school; in fact, he was a poetry major in college. He was so passionate about the Nasty Pig brand and his community that he realized he needed to become a businessman and started learning everything he could about numbers. He was determined to succeed, and he engaged a support system to help him. Over the years David worked with consultants not only to manage his bookkeeping but also to plan his cash for the upcoming months and find a way to not be afraid of the numbers. One of the most important things a creative mind can do is learn to understand the numbers and use them for decision making. So, David did exactly that.

This man manages his business like a true CEO and a true entrepreneur: he determines the best direction for his company, delegates what needs to be done to reach its goals, and constantly monitors its progress. Being a clothing brand is not an easy business (I mean, what is?) and to do it well you must keep your eyes on several factors: marketing, brand awareness, making a great product, and—last but not least—having enough cash flow every month to cover all your costs.

David didn't get to be a top-notch CEO all on his own (none of us do; if it looks like we do, it's an illusion). Throughout the years he had a burning desire to "make it" and a support team—consultants like me as well as a business coach—to serve as sounding boards and voices of reason. Now, you may not be able to hire a support team quite yet and that's okay. In part two, you will learn more about how to know when you need to hire advisors—and which ones to hire. Right now we'll look at how to assemble a small group of people who can show you your blind spots and make sure you are using relevant information and assumptions for business decisions.

I am not talking about friends and family, necessarily; I am referring to people you know, with whom you are not competing, who have been successful in their businesses and are willing to help you get there, too. Whom can you think of?

Recruit the right people.

Remember my client Frank, founder of D'Marie, of which I am proud to be a part? We will talk a bit about Frank throughout this book, as I feel his journey as a start-up business idea may be very relevant to you. He set up an advisory board right from the start, before he even launched. He assembled five to seven people to bounce ideas off, to give him advice on the next steps, and to point out what he was not seeing.

One of the advisors was my firm. I set up some accounting and tax priorities; my firm also pulled some financial projections together for seeking investor capital, which was part of the business plan. Another advisor was our then-mutual client, Michael, who built his agency and photoshoot management business from the ground up. Michael taught Frank the intricacies of contracts, dealing with brands and large companies, as well as their attorneys, which helped Frank tremendously.

If you are raising capital (more on this in the next few chapters) or are going after an agile market, you will need help. Don't make the mistake of thinking that you can go it alone, but that doesn't mean you have to split the ownership interest with someone else. Plenty of people will be genuinely eager to help you and volunteer their time to assist with your launch. Ask specific questions and set precise meeting goals, and that will be a great start.

Don't just say, "I need help, I don't know what to do." That will not help your advisors help you. Do a lot of background work so that you can meet with someone and say,

"I am thinking of doing this and that to launch, and this other thing to market—what do you think?" Or throw a brainstorming party to bounce off ideas and further analyze your options. You will be surprised how many people will show up to support you, absolutely free, because we want to be a part of the success of people we care about. Just do the prep work and your due diligence first. Remember one thing: The real danger in business and its back office (money, numbers, and tax matters) is not knowing what you don't know. This can compromise your future success, so take good care of your back office.

It will be to your advantage to meet with your board, together or one-on-one, monthly or quarterly. Ask for specific, solicited feedback. When making business moves, run them by the right people and you will be in better shape and make fewer mistakes along the way. And, yes, you will absolutely make mistakes. One of the goals of this book is to minimize the dollar cost of those to you.

Who would be a good candidate for the board?

On your board, you want someone who:

- has their finances under control, and
- has a track record of solid business profits, or
- has been a successful investor and is willing to share tips about what it takes to be an investment-worthy company.

You probably want a serial entrepreneur on your advisory board, too. So, someone who has launched a business or two (or three) and has been around the block a few times. Maybe a friend or a former colleague, or someone in your community?

You don't need a full board right away; you *can* assemble it slowly and over time. Give yourself space to find the right people who are willing to help you.

A word of caution: Don't spill your guts out to every potential board member. Be careful and protect your idea; do your due diligence on the person, too. Ask them questions, such as "what do you wish you had known before you started your business or project?" and "what's the one thing you regret doing and not doing?" and "if you could talk to your earlier self, what would you recommend addressing first?"—you get where I am going with this, right?

If having a board of advisors is good, though, is having a partner even better? You might not like what I am about to tell you.

5

Should You Have a Partner?

THIS CHAPTER WAS originally going to be titled "Partnerships Never Work." For more than fifteen years I've seen a lot of good and bad breakups, and, in the end, they cost all parties involved much more than they thought they "hedged" in the beginning, both financially and emotionally. In all my years, I have only seen one or maybe two companies with partnerships that worked well. Just occasionally they do work, but people are going to want to form partnerships regardless of my opinion. Because when we face uncertainty, whether it's risking money, respect, or whatever else is important to us, we sometimes feel that having a partner, a buddy, in business makes it a whole lot easier. It doesn't feel as lonely. And we think that we can share the risk.

So, let's examine a couple of breakups—but later in the book you will see some successes, too. If you know that you want to go it alone and have not thought about getting a partner, you *can* skip this chapter. (Why would you, though? It's a fun one.)

Partnership Is Like Marriage

Partnering with someone in business means a whole lot more than just splitting the risks and the "downside." It means dealing with the same person several times a day about every little thing. In the beginning we are often full of enthusiasm and excitement for the future (just like in a marriage), but as the time goes by we evolve, change, know more about the other person, and, ultimately, sometimes feel disappointed or angry, especially when times are tough.

Also just like in a marriage, you cannot know how the other person's aspirations and vision may change; you cannot be sure that other human being will share the exact same vision for the business as you do or have the same level of commitment and resources.

Consider Angela's story before you make any decisions.

Angela, a long-time friend, is a gifted graphic design executive and has built a business providing unique designs for some of the top agencies in the country. After she left her corporate job, she partnered with an acquaintance, Anthony, who seemed to have his stuff together. He set up an office, hired a few people, and in the meantime, managed a couple of other businesses and partnerships.

Angela's team did great work; clients were happy, money was flowing. At the time, and we are talking over a decade ago, I was one of the bookkeepers on the team. Angela was not very involved with the financial matters and completely trusted her partner. It turned out he wasn't all that trustworthy. Anthony got carried away by investor money flowing into one of his start-up ideas and sucked funds away from all the other entities he co-owned—without even asking.

Needless to say, the breakup was ugly. What Anthony had done surfaced when one of the agency's former employees

called Angela for the third time about the retirement contri-
bution she was entitled to and hadn't yet received because
there was no money. Things spiraled downward immediately
and got messy—not on Angela's part, on Anthony's. His ego
had been questioned. He got carried away by the slim chance
of his new venture being the "next Facebook," and he even
tried to blame it all on Angela. The situation left a scar on
Angela for quite a while.

Truth be told, Angela never needed a partner in business.
She is a super-intelligent, creative mind, capable of pushing
through the toughest times and coming out dry on the other
side. It seems that a lack of confidence in financial management drove her to rely on someone else to manage that
department, as she voluntarily relinquished control of it.

But Angela's journey wasn't over with that last breakup.
After that terrible experience, she went on and founded her
own design company—by herself. As I was involved with
bookkeeping and accounting, I knew that it was a much better setup, completely controlled by her alone. And then, a
few years later, she had a brilliant business idea for a gadget
design that became super-popular. The product was absolutely genius . . . but a new struggle was about to begin.

Because we are good people, we genuinely want to share
our successes with others. So did Angela, and she involved a
few cousins in this venture. It, again, seemed easier to "do
it" with other people. But the partnership quickly got out of
hand: the business needed cash infusions to sustain its hyper-
growth, and Angela and her husband were the only ones who
could afford to contribute. They were also the only ones motivated to make this business a success story.

After about three years of the couple running the business
and others being partners on paper, another cash infusion
was needed. This time Angela and her husband decided to

request that everyone equally contribute the needed funds. The other partners, faced with a significant cash requirement, folded and forfeited their interests.

This *was fair*, if you think about it: if they could not participate in times of need, why should they benefit from the upside, if and when the business got over the hurdle? And more than that: the two managing partners did everything possible to push this business forward, bent over backward to make it happen, while the others sat back, watched, and did nothing. This seemed unfair to Angela and her husband, and rightfully so. The breakup got pretty ugly, with threats and nasty comments coming from some of the other partners, which caused my clients significant anxiety, stress, and fear of a lawsuit.

Stories like Angela's happen quite often and they are rarely made public, but now you know that it could happen to anyone. Trying things out on your own is often scary, but let this book serve as your support system.

Think Twice Before Partnering Up

When money (or the potential for *a lot of money*) is on the horizon, some of our worst qualities may surface. It takes courage to stick to doing "what's right," and some people were just not raised that way. Also common is for new businesses with more than one main owner to split the functions among them based on who's stronger at something that the other dislikes. Finances and back-office fundamentals in particular are tempting to offload onto a partner. Don't do it!

Anyone can handle finances—in fact, everyone *must* know the basics, and this book will make sure that *you* do. The biggest mistake of people working in partnership with someone is to say, "I am not good at math. Finance is not my strength and I will let my partner deal with it while I deal with the business." That is a trap! Don't fall for it! *Especially* if you are not in the business alone, challenge yourself to understand and handle your back-office fundamentals. You will thank me later.

Just to press the point, I'll tell you two more stories of how people I know fell into that trap.

Who deserved what?

Alex and Jim were partners in an IT service company, CGIT, which provided hardware and software network support to accounting firms and other professional service businesses. The premise was that, instead of one company hiring an in-house IT person for $60,000 to $80,000, several smaller firms hired CGIT to perform "on demand" service for $20,000 to $30,000.

Alex and Jim spent many years together and built the business from the ground up. During that time, their lives evolved differently: Alex was single, with no children, and Jim had an autistic child who required a lot of attention. Alex could spend a lot more time at work, and Jim wanted to spend more time at home.

At the same time, the partners split their business duties: Alex oversaw back office (accounting, bookkeeping, paying bills, invoicing clients) and scheduling, while Jim performed some sales and management functions. Jim distanced himself from the financial side of things, and that was his big mistake. The predictable happened. Can you guess what?

In a few years the partners of CGIT found themselves in an "interesting" situation. The company's profits declined because of an economic downturn (and also a lack of proper attention to customer satisfaction), and it turned out that Alex had been taking money from the firm, because he thought it was rightfully his for all the hard work he had been putting in. Jim, on the other hand, was so busy at home that he took his eyes off the business ball and let new sales leads slip through the cracks while not paying enough attention to finances.

It got ugly pretty quickly. (Did you see that coming?) Jim discovered that Alex had been *bleeding* cash out of the business and Alex didn't feel like he had done anything wrong. That year, when I worked on filing their taxes, their firm experienced huge turmoil and they eventually closed its doors.

This outcome could have been avoided—it *should* have been avoided. Don't ever think that if you're the talent, a visionary, or the "creative one" in the mix, you don't have to deal with money. In fact, because you can envision a better world, you are obliged to learn about the numbers to make it happen. I'm not saying you should become an accountant—no way. I *am* saying that you need to be comfortable with looking at your sales, expenses, and net profits, and to make numbers-backed decisions. Make it your personal goal to regularly review and understand your numbers, and know the basics of your tax obligations. You can protect yourself from losing a lot of money for nothing.

Sometimes it gets even worse.

Charlie and his partner, Ben, had a successful, small fence-production and installation business. They'd been in business together for years. They had a warehouse in a New York suburb and were making good money, but they never seemed to have any reserves or extra money to take home. Ben handled the back-office matters, and their company's QuickBooks Online file, which Charlie had access to but rarely used.

One beautiful early autumn morning Charlie arrived at the warehouse to find it completely emptied out: all the tools, materials, and equipment had been taken (apparently at night); his QuickBooks Online access was no longer working; and Ben was nowhere to be found. A few months later he received a call from the IRS saying that he owed more than $100,000 for the prior quarter's payroll taxes, which were unpaid. (And the government is a stickler about payroll taxes that you withhold from your employees and don't remit to them.) Charlie had no idea how this had happened. He was speechless.

Charlie is a sweet person, upbeat and positive. Despite what his former partner did to him, Charlie didn't let the experience stop him. Instead, he started another business and worked out a plan to pay off the debt, because he believes Ben never will and Charlie just doesn't want the bad karma. He believes that what goes around comes around. Recently, Charlie won a large government service contract and is doing well. He is on his way to settle that debt he inherited and is building up his current business by himself. But imagine for a moment where Charlie would have been if he had started his first business without a partner. Imagine how far he could have been at the time when he had to start over.

What Should You Do?

When you feel anxious about starting a business, try to keep a cool head and do the following exercises before you shake hands on a partnership. Answer these questions for yourself and write down the answers (in a journal or Excel sheet or on a notepad).

Question 1: Why do I need a partner?

Ask yourself why you think you need a partner. Is it because you are going into business for the first time and aren't sure how to set it up? Are you trying to share risks with another person so it doesn't seem as scary? Do you not have enough money to launch? Are you concerned that you will run out of money before you "make it"?

Here's the deal. In later chapters this book will help you understand ahead of time whether you have enough funds to start and will provide you with the tools to make your idea happen with a minimum money investment. This, in turn, will give you confidence and you will know whether you can do it on your own.

Sharing risks with another person may seem comforting in the beginning but, boy, can it come back to bite you later. As you have seen in Charlie's story, there are many dishonest people with no integrity, and Angela's story proves to us that going into business with friends and/or family often brings out the worst in people, especially when the money is scarce.

You may have validated your idea, and it could be an exciting one, yet it could also require a significant investment of expertise, money, or time you don't have. Take a tech start-up for example: if you are not a software developer, you will need to pay someone to build your idea into a product, and with the current abundance of tech ideas, very often the folks benefiting are the programmers and developers rather than their clients. So, for tech start-ups, sometimes, a strategic partnership is needed. If that's your situation, let's look at some homework you need to do before you dive in.

Question 2: Do our visions align?

When you have found a potential partner for your venture, talk to them. You heard me right: t-a-l-k t-o t-h-e-m. Share your visions with each other: do they align? Discuss failure scenarios and listen to your future partner: How will they handle failure? What are their plans for life? Do they have a family they support and need to make it happen no matter what, or are they a world traveler?

Quite a few personality assessments out there can help you determine the type of person you are looking for based on certain traits that will complement yours. McQuaig is one of the most powerful assessments I have seen, but it's not the only good one. Your partner may want to take the test, too! This will give you both an understanding of whether your temperaments match and take the guesswork out of the process. Investing a few hundred bucks may save you thousands of dollars in disputes, legal fees, and anxiety in years to come.

Question 3: Have I got my papers together?

By now, you may have picked up subtle hints that I am not a fan of partnerships. In my accounting practice I have seen too many partnerships end in ugly breakups. These are painful for all parties involved, and it breaks my heart every time to see good people struggle. Relationships get ruined, money gets wasted, and disappointment persists.

Should you decide to take on a strategic partner, or if you already started with a partner, do your homework—and get a partnership agreement. This agreement can and should be prepared by an attorney and reviewed by your partner's attorney, too. You should read it in full, but at the minimum read the "worst-case scenario" sections so that you know what could happen and what your remedy is. This is probably the best thing you can do for yourself if you are going in with a partner.

Now, even if you don't want a partner—or even if you do— you may still want other people's money. Or do you? Let's see about that next.

6

Should You Get Investors?

MORE THAN A decade ago, when I had a successful bookkeeping practice and was just starting out as an accountant, I worked for a design firm. I handled its invoicing, regular bookkeeping, and reconciliations. The company had several entities and the owner had a true entrepreneurial mind. He also had a huge ego. Remember Anthony from Angela's story? Let's look at his side of the story.

Just about two decades ago the notion of a start-up was in its infancy and people across the globe were devising ideas to become the "Googles" and the "Facebooks" of the world. It reminded me of the gold rush of the mid-nineteenth century: people were obsessed with getting rich quick. Some did, in fact, find gold and get rich. And there were many ancillary beneficiaries—just like the people selling shovels for digging. This "start-up rush" era of the early 2000s reminded me to watch out for the ancillaries, and in Anthony's case, overseas programmers were definitely the "shovel-sellers."

Anthony's idea was to create a platform for bringing together movie and theater talent to collaborate with producers in creating bestselling performances. Although this was a great idea initially, Anthony used investor money. And what do you think happens when you spend someone else's money? That's right: nothing seemed too expensive, and he just kept spending.

Anthony ended up at the point of no return. He had been carried away by this pretty picture he had in his head and had started stripping his primary businesses of all their money. Someone *had* to pay the programmers to keep perfecting the platform. (I hope you can sense the note of sarcasm.)

Initially, the project raised about $1 million of committed capital. Needless to say, after half of it had flown out the door to the programmers for their services, the investors pulled out and the project never launched. Anthony's other businesses suffered tremendously and many had to shut down completely. Along the way, Anthony made several fatal mistakes. In addition to being carried away by the flow of investor funds, he took his eyes off his main business. He ignored the problems that were presenting themselves and operated under the belief that he was one launch away from repaying the investors—and the debt—and becoming rich.

Anthony is not alone. I bet you know someone who knows someone who has done something similar. So many people dive into an idea, especially with investor capital, with absolutely no plan of where that money will go. Seeing an entrepreneur's ego carry them away to neverland is heartbreaking.

It's not unusual for start-ups and for entrepreneurial minds to want to seek funding for their idea. As an accountant, I've witnessed many clients seeking funding but who could almost never pinpoint the real reason they wanted it. Sometimes I had to dig deep and ask a lot of questions to get to that reason. For many almost-preneurs and entrepreneurs, investor capital is the end goal, the ultimate finish line. They don't have a plan for becoming profitable or building a company that will leave a legacy.

I want *you* to do better and be smarter than that. For that reason, let's take a look at what you need to learn before you consider investor capital. Even if you have no plans to use investor cash, read this. It's interesting. And you might later decide a cash infusion would come in handy after all.

A Funded Company with No Profit and No Purpose

Many years ago, my husband and I were struggling financially, barely making ends meet. I had quit my full-time job when I got pregnant and started building my accounting practice. When our children were born, I spent a lot of time with them. Although we had to manage our finances carefully to live on less, I am happy to have done it this way. Eventually, I decided to get a full-time job for a year to get out from under. I am an entrepreneur at heart, so my plan was to continue to manage my own business on the side. Sometimes you do what you've got to do.

One interesting opportunity came up: to be the controller of a funded start-up producing new-generation footwear. At the interview, I spoke with the manager, Christy, who was excited that an experienced person was interviewing for the role. Christy mentioned that the company had outgrown the outside accounting firm they used to help manage its finances.

"We just secured our second round of funding, over $14 million," she said.

"All right, that's nice," I thought to myself, "They can afford to hire me." My ego was talking loud—I was curious, and the next step was talking to the CEO.

The CEO, Jack, was an energetic man in his forties, evidently excited about his company and passionate about his product. We had a high-level discussion. I talked about how I help clients grow and become successful; he talked about how his company was "awesome" and had a bright future ahead.

"Are you profitable?" I asked.

"Huh? What do you mean?"

"Is the company *profitable*?" I repeated. "Funding is nice, but are you actually making money?"

Jack blanked out for a moment. "We are not scheduled to be profitable until year four!" he exclaimed.

What happened next was probably not my best moment in an interview.

"Really?" I said. "You secured so much in funding but aren't making money?" I'm pretty sure my eyebrows raised high enough to touch the ceiling.

"Well, we just crossed a $10 million top-line sales mark!" Jack said. He shifted in his chair and began to fidget with the pens on his desk.

"Okay, and you are not profitable, right?" I couldn't help myself; the prudent accountant in me was shocked. I think my face gave away how I felt about this, because I didn't get the job. It was for the best.

So many companies have zero idea why they need funding, how they will use the money, and how they are going to *stay* in business and make it self-sufficient. If you are looking for funding, have a plan for the funds. Will you use them to boost your company so that it can gain momentum and then sustain it, or will you use the funds to make ends meet?

When investors fund projects like Jack's, I question their motives—and, frankly, their intelligence. It's possible that, in this case, there were many small investors, so no one really looked at the company's plan for the overall capital commitment. That business still happens this way is shocking to me. Jack's company still exists, and I can't help but wonder how they are managing money—whether it is profitable or not.

Profitability is merely an indicator, a litmus test, if you will. A deeper meaning of profitability comes down to a company's *purpose*, and that's bigger than money. Purpose is the underlying driver of a venture's success, and it goes beyond a simple passion for what you do. Purpose is rooted in your "why," as in why you started this business. Money is great, but a true brand has a purpose, a goal of influencing and, possibly, building a legacy. Also, most brands that know their purpose and intended impact develop a way of operating in a socially responsible manner.

Jack's company lacked that deeper purpose. I didn't feel it coming across when I spoke with him that day. He had secured a ton of other people's money and didn't consider the long-term impact of his company—at least, it wasn't at all obvious to me that he did. It seemed that purpose was lost among the dollar signs. "No skin in the game" certainly seems like the culprit here, which is why you may want to reconsider investor funding as your primary goal. Don't get me wrong, investor funds could be helpful—but only if you know exactly what your "why" is and how these funds will get you there.

Investor Funding Options

Among the various options for raising capital available to you, two of the most sought-after are angel investors (angels) and venture capitalists (VCs). Angels typically invest less than $1 million, and although they usually want to give you some advice, they do not want control over your business. They want *you* to develop *your* vision. VCs, on the other hand, invest millions and want a big chunk of your company in exchange. They also want to tell you how to run it and they bring their expertise and resources to the table.

Remember my client Frank and his start-up, D'Marie, which became a social media analytic tool? Initially he approached investors to pay for his development and launch. He consulted with a large, Boston-based law firm that believed in his idea and accepted him into their program. In addition to all the "freebies" they provided, they required him to purchase expensive directors and officers insurance, which he now realizes he didn't need at the time, so he wasted some money. As time went by his "why" developed and his approach has changed.

Back then, Frank was actively looking for capital. He pitched to more than 120 angels and VCs and secured a tiny (compared to other start-ups that were funded at the time) angel investment. These funds enabled him to continue to pursue and further develop his dream. A decade into the business and his competition was no longer in the market. Pretty impressive, I say.

"You have to ignore what others advise, especially if they are not the ones writing a check," Frank explained. "At first, I listened to everyone eager to give suggestions, but then I asked a few of those people: 'If I incorporate these changes, would you invest your money into this business?' And *poof*! Just like that, they disappeared."

As a boring accountant in recovery, I don't like the idea of using someone else's capital. It removes that "skin-in-the-game" component and often relieves you of the responsibility to make it no matter what. New entrepreneurs don't always know why the money is needed, and once you get the funds, you may feel inclined to go all in and get carried away by the "top-line revenue," just like Jack did. Inevitably, your attitude toward, and your focus on, your business shifts and you won't necessarily make great business decisions. That's where even seasoned entrepreneurs have to be careful. The ones who make it, like Frank, keep minding their financial decisions despite investor capital. When Frank did not get vc funding after two years of trying, I was relieved, in a way: It wasn't (then) clear to me what this money would do or how it would be used, and the fact that his idea wasn't funded "big" meant it needed further work. The angel funding he did secure was perfect for him.

During an interview for this book Frank mentioned something that surprised me. He said, "I believe everyone needs to look for funding."

"Really? Why?" I asked. I remained skeptical.

"You have to be able to sell your idea to at least one person; two or three is better. It's a validation checkpoint for your launch. They have to believe in you and your business. If you cannot convince anyone to invest in your idea, guess what? It's not a great idea."

I couldn't believe my ears. It's a pretty bold thing to say, but I have to admit: Frank's position makes sense. To have your idea validated by the market is an important and even critical step. This is why many product-based start-ups launch through crowdfunding.

Crowdfunding is a way to validate your idea, and also to get some initial funding without giving up any ownership of your company. (Kickstarter and Indiegogo are two of the most famous platforms for crowdfunding.) An important part of this journey is being very clear about why you need that money and what it will do for your business. You will need to record a top-quality video and tell your viewers a story. Check out *Building a StoryBrand* by Donald Miller to help clarify your message, as for crowdfunding to be successful you need to do this.[1] If you don't get crowdfunded, take it as a sign that your idea needs more work.

With this type of capital funding, you also need to offer rewards for various levels of commitment. On many of these platforms it's an all-or-nothing deal. You have to get your goal fully funded (or overfunded) or you get none of the money. Keep that in mind as you set your funding goal. Interestingly, my firm has worked with clients whose main business was selling items on Kickstarter. Those folks nailed the offering campaign and product, and had successful programs, several of them per year, of limited-edition unique products. So that may be an option for you, too.

Raise Investor Funds, if That's Right for You

If you want to be successful at raising investor funds, you have got to come prepared and leave nothing to chance. You do have options. Many major cities and major universities have incubators where you can meet with and pitch to a number of investors in a short period of time. You can also try to find your way to one of the bigger angel groups.

One of these groups, New York Angels, is fairly well known and is behind some successful start-ups. One of their board members, Brian Cohen, wrote a book titled *What Every Angel Investor Wants You to Know*, in which he describes exactly what their group looks for in a start-up—you may want to check it out. One key point that made a lot of sense to me as an accountant is, as Cohen says, "If you give me a choice between investing in an 'A' team with a 'B' idea, and a 'B' team with an 'A' idea, I'll take the 'A' team every day of the week."[2] Something to consider, don't you think?

Remember in chapter 4 we talked about getting your group of geniuses together? It becomes even more important to find people who will pull you up, who will be as passionate about your idea or project as you are. You don't necessarily need to spend a ton of money right away. If you have a few specific people in mind and you're sure that they are A players, see if you can barter with them or find another way of compensating them while you're fleshing out your pitch to the investors. Maybe offer them stock options as a reward or barter for a service. Early into my practice I bartered for stock options as well as services to get what I needed and couldn't afford at the time. This strategy will not always work, but it doesn't hurt to try.

To successfully pitch your idea to investors, you will also need a business plan. Numerous software options and online resources can help, and since new ones come out fairly often, I recommend that you search for the one that makes a lot of sense to *you*. And just like with anything else, in this step you will need to face your numbers. You will need to come up with projected numbers. Yup. And it will be painful, for sure. Running rough numbers will help you expose your bold assumptions and understand the real picture of your profit, costs, and break-even point. We will dig into this in chapter 9, but if you need the template now, go to dreamboldbook.com to download the spreadsheet to get started. Budget is a super-important part of the business plan and you will want to do it right.

Next, let's look at a few issues to keep in mind.

Funding Operations with Investor Money

Do you remember Angela, burned several times by partnering with dishonest people, including Anthony, who we looked at again in this chapter? First an acquaintance, who became her partner, and later stole money from their joint business.

With that business, her only involvement in the finances was billing clients, so when the money bubble burst, it was a shock to her. Later, with her own firm, which was wildly successful, she kept an eye on the top line—gross revenues—and "sort of knew" the bottom line. It was her third business, the business with her cousins, that really put her financial management skills to the test.

Angela's third business struggled from day one. Since she developed a new product, she was certain that a lot of funds had to go toward advertising, to establish brand loyalty and recognition. Unfortunately, there was no budget and no control over that spend. Angela again focused on the top line: gross sales instead of how much was left at the end of the day. Her bottom line didn't go out of the red for years. She and her partner depleted their personal assets and were left in a vulnerable financial position.

After a few years, an angel investor came into the picture. He was a seasoned investor and quickly realized that the business needed cash and he was right. What he didn't know was that the funds were not managed well. There was no strategy, no advertising budget, no fast decision making given the changing day-to-day sales environment. Management focused on the product and line development instead of money and expense management. Angela defaulted to managing by putting out fires, concentrating on the most pressing matter of the day. The advertising spend was through the roof and without control or return on investment (ROI) analysis done on it.

Angela's investor threw in several hundred thousand dollars and provided some valuable guidance to her, but nothing changed dramatically because the funds were used in advertising and operations instead of on growth and drastic improvements. The business grew the top line dramatically over time, but it was not profitable for a second and did not bring any of the money back to the people involved.

My engagement with Angela's company ended after several years of working together. I attempted several times to help her realize the importance of numbers and wasn't successful. I expect her business to function on life support until the investor money runs out. It's harsh but true. Angela's biggest mistakes were using investor money to fund operations long term, not reining in advertising, and not planning ahead. She never became comfortable with looking at all the numbers regularly while we worked together—there was always a reason not to. Yet, things could have been different for her. Had she created a cash forecast, set a strict budget for advertising, and determined the level of return on ad spend (ROAS is the term), she would have either closed her doors after two years and started something new or would have built a lean business by now.

Angela's story could be anyone's, even yours. Saying you are "not good at math," or some version of that, to take responsibility off your shoulders is easy, but it's a trap. When working with investors, you must know how you will spend every penny you seek. No exceptions. It could be used for the first few months of operation, but it must come with specific goals and milestones for your business to reach for it to make sense to the investor and to you.

When You Think About Investor Capital

When you are deciding whether to seek any kind of funding, consider the following questions in light of the real company examples from this chapter.

Question 1: Why am I looking for funding?

Do I need to show specific initial capital to a franchisor (a company that gives you a license to use their name and business model)? It's often the case that franchises ask for specific initial capital to allow you to get a franchise license from them, so this is a very good reason you may want to look for money. Many years ago my friends Yulia and Andrey sought an initial loan or funding to pursue their dream of opening up a franchised dance studio in New York, and the franchisor required proof of a pretty high sum of money in their business account. This couple was able to secure funding and they have been successfully operating their dream studio for over a decade.

Question 2: Do I need to fund research and/or an initial study?

Research is another good reason to seek external funding. Take medical research as an example. Instead of taking on a partner, you may want to explore this option and seek out angel investors so that later you are not told how to run your business, which could be the case with a VC investor.

Question 3: How much do I need?

You must determine how much you need before you seek funding. This goes back to your "why" because the amount of funds you seek for operations (as opposed to an initial money boost) can vary significantly. Your marketing message (your pitch) will also depend on it, so you better have all your ducks in a row. Your plan must feel and look solid to you and to a potential investor.

Question 4: Do I have a schedule for spending the money I raise?

This is just a continuation of the previous question and goes well with chapter 9. When you plan your business's first twelve months of operations, you will have a clear picture of how much money you need. You will also see if and when your business is scheduled to generate a profit and sustain itself. You don't want to always need investor funds, right? See earlier in this chapter where I discuss funding operations with investor money.

Question 5: Is my search for funding to feed my ego or to get me where I couldn't go without it?

This is a tough-love question and is probably the most important one of all in this section. Look deep down into your heart and understand what you feel. Ask yourself why, and just let the question marinate for a few days; give your brain some time to offer you a solution. Understand that, as cliché as this may sound, there is no such thing as a free lunch and you will pay for the money either with loss of control or with your own sanity. The exercise of searching for funding will help you refine your business model and clarify your message to both your potential investors and potential customers, so it's definitely worth exploring. But know your "why" first.

Question 6: Am I just looking to sell my idea?

You may be looking for funding because you just want to sell your idea and cash out. There is absolutely nothing wrong with that! Be up front about it and you may find someone who is interested. If you just want to sell your idea, then you are in a different business: the idea-selling business. Consider just nailing your elevator pitch and getting in front of a bunch of investors.

One thing you should be aware of, though, is that investors are more likely to invest in a well-built or well-run business than to just buy an idea. Ideas are everywhere now—there is an abundance of them—but turning an idea into a successful business is an art and a skill. Remember the preference of the New York Angels' Brian Cohen? He'll always take an "A" team over an "A" idea? If you're still determined to do it, I challenge you to come up with three reasons why an investor should give you money. What's in it for them?

What's Next?

We are getting close to the core of this book, the "meat" if you will. So, I want to warn you about something. There is a pretty high likelihood that once you have done all the work of the prelaunch planning, you will find that you do not wish to pursue your idea at this moment, and I want to tell you (again) that that is *okay*. It's better to discover that *now* rather than a couple of years into it, not making money and feeling stuck.

You may be reading this book because you know that someday you will want to call the shots of your own life and be your own boss. With the stories and tools I share with you, you will be able to start and manage *any* business in the future. You need to test your ideas to determine the right business for you, and it may take a few goes. Give yourself some time and space to come up with a solid idea and a plan. You will thank yourself later.

Now, if you are ready to launch, let's see how to do this right, avoid mistakes, skip the anxiety, and secure your dream.

PART TWO
START SMART

7

Step One: Create Your Legal Entity

F IRST OF ALL, congratulations! By now I bet you have done some serious thinking. You have validated your business idea, planned what your business will look like, and made a few important decisions about partnerships and investor capital. That alone is a ton of work and if you have made it this far, hopefully, things are getting clearer.

Once you are ready to launch, you will inevitably wonder whether or not to incorporate or organize another entity. In my tax practice, that's one of the most frequent things I am asked about. It's a question people often end up taking to the internet.

This chapter is specific to U.S. taxation; however, the approach may be applicable in other countries. You will need to engage a specialist who can perform a similar analysis for your business if it is not based in the United States. Also, remember, here we only look at *active* small businesses—an actual business as opposed to, say, an investment in real estate or other activity that's usually passive. So, the material presented here is with that in mind.

Entity selection is probably the most important decision you will make as you're starting out because it impacts how much you will pay in taxes, whether you will have to reorganize later to match investor expectations, and a few other considerations. If you've already formed an LLC or have been freelancing under your own name, this chapter will help you clarify what entity is right for you, so that you can adjust and potentially save yourself money on taxes. My personal approach to life has always been to make decisions today that leave me a choice for tomorrow. I apply the same approach to the process of selecting an entity, but first we need to review a few important concepts because they will play a role in your entity choice. Let's get to it.

If You Aren't Sure You're Ready to Make It Official

Often, the entity decision doesn't have to happen right away. It depends on whether you have partners, whether you're looking for capital, in which state you will be operating, what your three- and five-year goals are, and what your liability exposure is. If you are at a stage where you want to *try things out first*, you may want to operate as a sole proprietor—in other words, not organize *any* entity right away, and just freelance for a while. Doing so will allow you to test the waters and understand the immediate demand for your product. If you are in the service industry, freelancing in the beginning, and possibly still holding down a job, will give you some time to figure things out while keeping your peace of mind.

Can You Rely on Your Accountant?

Over the past fifteen years I've been heartbroken several times—just not the way you may think. Every time I get into a tax discussion at a kid's birthday party or a friend's barbecue, there is someone who realizes that the voice inside telling them that they're paying too much in tax was right. Usually, it's because they never really checked whether that LLC (probably the most common entity formed, discussed later in the chapter) was the right choice for them. A situation like that can be "fixed" going forward, so it's not the end of the world, but people get upset because, for all those years, they could have had more money left in their own pockets. Seeing that realization in their eyes breaks my heart, every time.

The truth is that modern accountants who practice in a traditional style almost never spend enough time with a business owner to provide advice that goes beyond occasional, specific questions and comments about tax filing. Accountants are overworked and forced to take on a lot of clients to be able to provide a decent living for their families, only to find themselves in a never-ending race to keep up with work. Unfortunately, both professionals and clients pay the price for that and nobody is to blame.

Price pressure and the tight deadlines accountants deal with backfire for people like you, who desperately need good advice and support early on. As a result of the ongoing rat race, accountants feel uncomfortable charging for advice, and most of us know that when something is free, you get what you pay for. So, we rush to "check it off" our list and move on, and rarely sit down to talk with you about the impact your plans will have on your business or your future taxes. The result is also that people often don't even consult a professional and instead research online. Later in this book, we will examine the new generation of accounting advisors who have transformed their practices to be more client-focused. Certainly, that level of service costs significantly more than a traditional firm, but you are paying for a true business advisor and a partner in your corner, and that's priceless. This book will help you get some of the basics right and save money, so that you can later hire a good advisor—and can afford them.

Are You Throwing Money Away?

It is important for you to know that, in this chapter, we will only cover one choice for one entity. If and when you have several distinctive streams of income that could potentially be split into completely separate businesses, I urge you to seek a tax planner to possibly create a multi-entity structure for you. You can save hundreds of thousands of dollars in tax by doing it right.

This book and this chapter are not here to provide legal advice, but are meant to give you an idea, make you curious, and force you to think ahead. You see, the right entity for *you* will never be the same as for someone else. It depends on *your* vision and long-term goals for this business idea.

Usually, attorneys and internet search engines recommend starting an LLC (a limited liability company). An LLC is not a corporation, so you are not considered incorporated, but you are considered "organized" and do have limited liability protection. That means that if your businesses ever gets sued and has to pay up, generally, the plaintiff cannot go after your personal assets. An exception to that is if you did wrong on purpose: in that case, no entity can protect you from being personally liable.

When we talk about LLCs, there are two options: a single-member LLC (SMLLC, for short) and a multiple-member LLC (MMLLC), with two or more partners. From a tax perspective, LLC is one of the worst options, but so many people come to me with an LLC already formed and they don't know why. It is my hope that, if it is the right choice for you, it will be a conscious one.

I had known Josh for eight years, and he had never asked me to do his taxes. I was still in the mode of a traditional-style accountant, and getting more clients was my ultimate goal. He had quite a few real estate investments that he managed, and a few times I mentioned to him, jokingly, that "he should give me his tax business."

His response was always, "Well, my current guy, I've known him for twenty years, and he's pretty good, and he gives me a good deal on my filings."

The discussion ended there, because I don't negotiate on my fees; I don't have a conveyor-belt operation and we don't "crank out" returns at my firm. Every client we handle gets sufficient attention to make sure that they get the tax breaks available to them.

A few months after the last time we had that conversation, I got trained in tax planning. It's not the service you may be thinking of, so let me explain how it's different. It's not planning for *tax payment*, strategizing how and when to pay taxes you owe. It is developing and implementing a plan to use tax strategies that apply to you now or will do so in the future, so you can find ways to have to *pay less tax*. Tax planning also includes managing the paper trail and money trail related to those strategies so that it's not just a plan in theory and can be backed up.

I reached out to Josh about if he wanted me to review his taxes and books to see if anything was missed. He agreed, of course. I spent about an hour reviewing Josh's paperwork and found that he could have deferred about *$40,000* in federal tax in the prior year alone. Unfortunately, that opportunity was lost, since the window to make a retirement contribution was closed by the time I reviewed it. Josh was shocked, to say the least. Wouldn't you be? Further review found that because his entity was an LLC, Josh paid a ton of money in tax, whereas a simple upgrade to an S corporation (which we will cover later in this chapter) could have saved him a lot of money *year after year.*

Josh's story didn't end there. His then-accountant never did any due diligence on his business books, so bank, credit card, and other balances were never checked, verified, or balanced. As a result, out of $600,000 Josh earned in revenue for that year, $300,000 was subjected to the ordinary ("regular," higher) tax plus a self-employment tax of 15 percent, instead of the correct, *reduced* "capital gains" tax, which was appropriate. My rough calculations came up to about *$80,000* Josh overpaid in taxes that year.

Needless to say, Josh was shocked yet again. All this happened in mid-December and there was still a chance to take advantage of some of the benefits and get some money back for the previous and the current year. So, we did. Josh paid a pretty high price for my firm to go back and harvest the savings. I did a lot of work, but he was happy to pay because he was getting a lot of money back in return. You can only imagine how much he wished he could turn back time and switch to my firm sooner.

Cases like Josh's are *very* common, but I want to make one thing clear: in certain situations we will discuss later, an LLC may be the right choice for you, but generally a one-business entrepreneur organized as an LLC costs a lot of money in tax.

Would You Rather Be in Delaware?

It is my hope that by now you understand why first developing your end goal is important. Knowing your "space domination" goal is even more critical in this chapter. You don't want to find yourself overpaying taxes later, when you finally start making good money, so paying attention to it now can make a huge difference, and we will come back to this.

My client Terry developed a web-based valuation tool and my firm wasn't involved initially in the entity selection process, so he had a previously organized New York corporation. In our early conversations, I once asked him, "After you get to where you want to be in this business, do you want to sell it or keep running it forever? What will make you happy?"

"I want to just run it and provide a good living for me and those close to me," he said. So, we converted his company to an S corporation to take advantage of the tax benefits.

Later that year, Terry and I met with a law firm famous for their start-up expertise. They insisted on creating a Delaware corporation and merging the two entities to have one Delaware entity. Both Terry and I weren't convinced, but as it turns out Delaware's laws were more protective of a business, as the attorneys explained. They also suggested that limited liability protections provided by LLCs and corporations are taken very seriously by the Delaware courts, which is important at a time of a dispute or a potential lawsuit. Moreover, one of the attorneys insisted that if our ultimate goal was to get investor money, being a Delaware company gives potential investors confidence in case things go south. Well, that certainly made sense to us, so we let the firm do what was needed and, voilà, Terry had a Delaware corporation.

For you, the rule of thumb is as follows: If you are looking to launch several businesses in the near future, or if you are looking for investor funds, or if your ultimate goal is to eventually sell your business, you should consider organizing in the state of Delaware. If that's what you decide to do, keep three things in mind. First, you will need to get authority to do business in the state in which you will operate (generally, your home state). It's not a big deal and the filing company will take care of that—just let them know. Second, every year you will need to pay Delaware what's called a franchise tax (for corporations). Again, it's not a big deal and the filing company can handle that for you annually. Third, you will need to have a registered agent with a Delaware address. All that means is that there should be a mailing address in Delaware for you to receive any kind of legal documents. And again, the filing company will help you with that.

What's a filing company? It's any one of many companies that provide an organization service. They create and dissolve entities, handle all the related filings, and make the process seamless and easy for you. Like I said, you need to tell them what you want, and you have the three important items covered in the previous paragraph.

If you are not planning on getting investor capital and are only launching this one business for now, it would make more sense to organize in your home state; you will spend less money and will have fewer things to worry about. Also, keep in mind that in certain countries in Europe, if you plan on dealing with them, companies organized in the states of Delaware and Wyoming are considered to be organized in offshore zones, which may prevent them from being able to do business with you.

Why Do Long-Term Goals Matter?

Becoming a corporation of any kind provides varying benefits and has drawbacks as discussed later in this chapter. At this time I want to challenge you to consider your own personal long-term goals, as well as your long-terms plans for the business that you're starting. Are you starting it to run it and live off the income? Or are you planning to sell it in the future and start something else?

Take your time with this question. It's important, because section 1202 of the Internal Revenue Code allows for a huge tax break if you sell your business after five years as long as the business is something called a C corporation (you'll learn more about this entity shortly). Section 1202 gives you a chance to pay zero tax on up to $10 million of gain (in other words, what you make on the business's sale). We will also discuss this when we look at the pros of a C corp, but it has some important downsides, too, so don't make this decision hastily.

Are There Local Taxes to Watch Out For?

My client Evan, an architect in New York City, has a small solo practice with a few junior architects. He has been very smart with money and has managed to keep his business lean. Evan knew another architect in the building, who was also a solo practitioner. They both worked with renovations and commercial projects and enjoyed their work but felt like they were limited in the size of projects they could pursue. So, they decided to collaborate and create a joint entity. My firm got involved with figuring out the best entity type for their venture. Their options—as I will tell you more about just

below—were an LLC (taxed as a partnership), an S corporation, or a C corporation. So I ran a few scenarios.

You see, New York City has its own tax for both corporations and unincorporated entities like LLCs. NYC also does
not recognize S corporations, so all companies getting any
benefit from doing business in the five boroughs of New York
City pay some kind of tax. Similarly, many localities around
the country have an additional tax. California, for example,
taxes LLCs and makes those much less favorable. In this book
I am focusing on federal tax effects, as they are usually more
impactful in terms of dollar amounts. Be sure to consider
state and local taxes together for the three primary options
we discuss, and consider the entire tax impact.

As for Evan and his partner, I ran scenarios solely in terms
of tax purposes. Given that the two architects already operated their own entities (LLCs) and would revenue-share on
joint projects based on hours and staff involved, my analysis proved that a C corporation would save both partners the
most and would provide for a possibility of a later tax-free sale.

When considering state and local taxes, you will need to
consult an accountant. The following decision matrix will
give you the best choice in terms of federal tax and is valid,
assuming there aren't major changes to the basics of the
entity laws.

The Decision Matrix

Don't be concerned if your vision and goals change along the
way. Knowing what you know now, you will course-correct if
you need to. Choose what's right for you *at this point in time*.
Everything can be fixed later (as long as you set things up so it
can), so give yourself some space and take it easy. Three main

points you have to consider when choosing the right entity for you are investors, partners, and your ultimate goal. I've made a decision matrix to show you the best choice on the basis of these factors.

Your main choices are a limited liability company, a C corporation, and an S corporation. Someone could argue that you could have a regular partnership or be a sole proprietorship (doing business under your name), but neither of these options gives you protection from someone suing you and going after your personal assets, like a home or a car. For any other scenario besides a one-person LLC, you will have a separate business tax filing every year.

Sam and Natasha worked together at a large media company in New York. They both enjoyed working in the industry, had pretty solid career growth, and built good contacts. A few months ago they decided to join forces and start a joint venture together. Naturally, they were trying to decide on the type of entity, and a free consultation with an attorney led them to choose an S corporation. Then they came to me.

Several conversations with Natasha and Sam proved that an S corporation was the wrong choice for them. Here is why. Sam was planning to keep his full-time job for at least a few years in the beginning. Natasha had just quit hers to devote her full attention to the new business. Sam was a single guy with no immediate plans to get married. Natasha was hoping to have kids within two or three years. Both Natasha and Sam had a few clients of their own that they planned on keeping, and they wanted to be able to sell their new agency at some point in the future.

This matrix is best done step by step. So let's take a look (see next page).

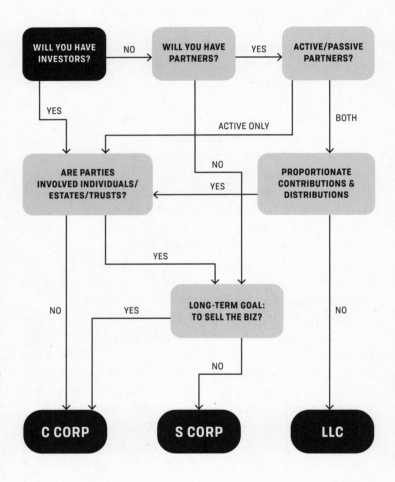

Step 1: Investors. Have you decided about investors (see chapter 6)? Select a "yes" or "no" arrow here. If you haven't made up your mind about investors yet, pick the option you're leaning toward. For Sam and Natasha the answer was "no."

Step 2: Partners. This relates to chapter 5. What did you decide about having a partner? Since Natasha and Sam are unrelated, aren't a couple, and were starting a business together, they picked "yes."

Step 3: Active and passive partners. In your business, will you have both active and passive partners, just active, or just passive? A partner can take an active role in the business: manage its operations, make decisions, hire others, and so on. Or a partner can be a passive partner, which really is more of an investor relationship, but the person holds an interest and can participate in profits. When one (or more) of the partners brings initial capital (money) and, maybe, personal connections into the business and is interested in earning income from that investment, while not wanting to be involved in the daily operations, you have a mixture of both active and passive partners, so pick "both." If partners will be actively involved in the business's daily operation, select "active only." I omit the "passive only" option because that will not be your business. That is just an investment, but we are talking specifically about you *running* a business. As for Sam and Natasha, they both planned to be actively involved in the business, so they moved along the "active only" line.

Step 4: The next item is proportionate distributions. This needs to be explained a bit. Will you and your partner(s) put money in and take money out based on the share of the business you own? You may be thinking, "Is there any other way?" The answer is yes. Here is an example.

Two partners get into a business together. One of them puts in $10,000 to keep the business going. The other partner brings their connections in the professional world plus their programming skills. They agree to split the ownership fifty-fifty. They agree that the second partner brings a lot more to the table. So, they decide to split any profit the business generates thirty-seventy for the first five years, while keeping their ownership interest at fifty-fifty. So, someone in this situation would have selected "no" and have gotten the LLC result. Conversely, if you and your partner were to invest money and time, and share risks and ownership evenly, then you'd choose "yes."

Step 5: A rule prohibits corporations and other legal entities from owning an S corporation; that's why this question is here. So, if at least one of the potential partners is already some kind of a legal entity, pick "no." Otherwise follow the "yes" line for this question, which is what I did for Natasha and Sam.

Step 6: Earlier we talked about considering your long-term goals for your business and for your life. Have you thought about it? This is where your "space domination" goal will come in handy, so take a moment to revisit your long-term goals. Are you thinking that someday you will sell this business? Or do you want to keep running it forever? If you are looking to sell it at some point, a terrific tax benefit is available for that, but you kind of have to decide when you are starting out. To be able to get this benefit you must remain a C corp for "substantially all of the... holding period of such stock" and be an active business.[1]

Sam and Natasha ended up with a recommendation for a C corporation (goal to sell), but their journey wasn't over yet. Now, let's look at a setup where several entities may be best.

Multitiered Structures

You could take advantage of the freedom a partnership-like setup allows and combine disproportionate contributions and distributions while still reaping the tax benefits of an S or a C corporation. This could be accomplished with a multitiered structure. In other words, a corporation could own a share of a partnership LLC. There are limitations to this setup, as well, which are beyond the scope of this book; and, frankly, you will need to involve an experienced tax planner to set this up for you correctly, considering all your goals and needs.

So, for Sam and Natasha, I recommended a joint C corporation, with each of them owning their own LLC. They would maintain their personal clients within their respective LLCs (taxed as S corporations), while their joint income would be within the joint C corporation.

The next few sections go over the pros and cons of the three main entity choices.

LLC Taxed as a Partnership

Pros

An LLC is often easier to launch than an S or a C corporation, although in some states it's more expensive. The beauty of an LLC is that it is easier for the entity to admit new partners, and also for individual partners to sell their interests if they want to cash out. This can be especially important if you are starting out as a sole owner and looking for strategic partners or investors.

An LLC is also a great option for situations when some partners are investing their time and expertise but not money, yet all share profits and losses according to certain percentages. For other entity types you often need to be a lot more careful with taking money out and investing money into the business.

Partnerships have special rules about when partners lend funds to the company. Most loans give "basis," or the amount of money you have at risk, to all partners equally. The notion of basis becomes important when a company is losing money (has tax losses) because it limits how much loss you can take in a given year. Imagine investing money into your business, losing a portion of it, and not being able to reduce your taxes because of your loss. That's terrible! So the higher the basis, the better, and loans in partnerships gives partners *additional* basis. This is not the case for other types of entities.

If one partner lends money to the entity, other partners benefit from it, even though only one is actually risking a loss. This is why partnership is the only entity that allows for disproportionate contributions and distributions, as long as the partners agree to it and there is a reason for it besides tax savings. So instead of lending money to the company, the "money" partner would contribute it to the partnership. This would give *that* partner all the benefit, as he or she is assuming all the risk.

Cons

As you now know, a partnership could have two partner types: *active*, which applies to partners involved in the day-to-day business and its management; and *passive*, who are "mere investors" and do not participate in any major decisions of the business.

In the beginning, especially if you have strategic partners who bring skills or money to the table, there is a high likelihood that your partners will be primarily active, which

creates self-employment tax on all the income. You are probably wondering, "Is that a good or bad thing?" The answer
is, "It depends." I know, totally lawyer-like response, but
let me explain. When you make money—in other words,
when you're profitable—an active partner will pay federal,
state, and possibly local income tax—in addition to an extra
15.3 percent self-employment tax on top of that. That means
you could end up paying more than 50 percent in tax. Not so
great, right? The flipside is that if you lose money (the business isn't profitable yet), being classified as active allows you
to take those losses and not have the "passive loss" limitation
to worry about. Passive income has its own taxation rules and
they are less favorable when it comes to losses. Keep in mind
that you cannot just flip the switch between active and passive
as you wish. That classification depends on facts surrounding
every partner's role, and you should document all the relevant events that happen during each year of business.

Part of your strategy can be to allow for a multilevel structure, as we have discussed. If you must have an LLC because
you have your heart set on it or because of disproportionate
money inflows or outflows, every partner or investor can get
their own entity (a C or an S corp), which, in turn, will own a
share of this "umbrella company," your *main* LLC. If this is
your scenario, you need the help of a tax planner to make sure
you have everything covered.

One thing to keep in mind: if you are going to get venture
capital funding, know that many VCs do not like to invest in
LLCs, so you will need to incorporate and be a C corporation. VCs and angel investors prefer a Delaware corporation
to invest in, according to author David S. Rose.[2] As you may
remember, Delaware could work for you because it has laws
favoring businesses, and has a special Court of Chancery,
which decides corporate law cases fairly quickly and without a

jury. But incorporating in Delaware may be a waste of money if you're not looking for investors.

C Corporation (C Corp)

C corporations are regular corporations, and we tax geeks call them C corps for short. Let's look at pros first.

Pros

C corps have a huge advantage for start-ups. The Internal Revenue Code section 1202 allows you to sell your company and pay no tax on up to roughly $10 million of profit (in other words, what you made on it). That's a whole lot of tax savings, but there are very strict rules you will need to follow. The corporation must be yours for at least five years and it has to be a C corp for the majority of the holding time. The tax savings could come to $2 million or more, so this is a big pro of C corps.

Another important pro is that you may keep the company's earnings, to a certain extent, within the entity and pay only the corporate tax on it. This becomes important if you are reinvesting the profit into the business to spur growth and are not taking it out for yourself for the time being. In contrast, in a pass-through entity like a partnership or an S corporation, you pay tax on all profits personally regardless of whether or not you have taken the funds out of the business or reinvested it back.[3] In a pass-through scenario, if you have earned a profit but left it in the company to be used for expansion, you will have to come up with funds on your own to pay your taxes.

The third benefit of a C corp is that it will work very well in a multitiered setup, especially when you have several distinct income streams. If set up right, you can reap all the benefits of a C corp and pass-through entities without the effects of the downside of each entity type.

Aviad and Ohad operated a dress showroom for several years. Their clients came to the showroom to see clothes and collections, and later placed orders. The showroom was chic, modern, and stylish and gained a lot of attention and respect in the fashion community. Several years later, because this power couple is unbelievably talented and creative, Aviad and Ohad developed their own brand of clothing, which was also prominently displayed and sold at their showroom. This brand quickly gained a *lot* of traction.

For a little while, before I got involved, the partners operated their new brand under the same entity, an LLC taxed as an S corporation. As their sales volume increased, they could no longer keep both businesses under one entity and there was a great opportunity to separate the brand into its own. So, we did a "spin-off" of the brand into a C corp, owned by the couple individually, so that Aviad and Ohad could sell it in the future, if they so wanted, and pay zero tax on up to $10 million each. That's $4 million in federal capital gains tax savings. The client is happy.

C corps take a bit of work every year to manage, but the benefits often far outweigh the time and monetary costs. A C corp also allows you to have different classes of stock (for example, preferred and common), which is great for when you seek investor capital, especially several rounds of it.

Cons

C corps bear some important cons, and the infamous "double taxation" is one of them. This entity is my favorite to use for a multi-entity structure but isn't great when it comes to a single-entity business. A C corp pays its own tax, including federal, state, and possibly local. The math doesn't quite work out as a straight double tax, but on a certain amount you end up taking for yourself, you will pay tax again personally—though, in many cases, at a preferential (in other words, lower) tax rate.

Another important con is that, in addition to having to prepare taxes for the entity separately, if the company is in its infancy and losing money, you cannot use that loss to pay less tax personally. The loss will be "paused" to be used later. You *will* get the benefit of all these expenses—not right away, but in the future, if and when you earn a profit.

Caution: if you have to close your doors before making a profit, you *will* claim your losses in that final year. The only downside is that it will be a capital loss. You're probably thinking, "Why do you say 'downside'?" Well, you can only "offset" any other personal income at $3,000 per year, one year at a time. So, if you invested $15,000 into this business venture and lost it, it might take you five years to deduct the loss completely. It's not the best scenario because paying less taxes today would be better than paying partially less for the next five years, but it is what it is, and you just need to be aware of it.

If this is your entity of choice because you are looking for significant investments, keep in mind that it will cost you some money in the beginning. Make sure you can afford it and are realistic about the likelihood of securing the investments.

Subchapter S Corporation (S Corp)

You may be thinking, "What does S corporation even mean?" Allow me to explain. All corporations are created as regular, or we call them C, corporations. Then you have two and a half months to file a piece of paper and elect this "special" status. The part of the law that takes care of all-things-S-corporation is called subchapter S, which is why the name S corporation stuck.

This is an important tool for a small business owner, and the benefits of it cannot be stressed enough. To be honest, S corps are secretly my favorite. Yes, it's a separate tax return to be filed, but, girl, do you get a lot of tax benefits and possibilities!

We are going to explore the effects of localities on entities next, but for the purposes of pros and cons we'll hold all other things equal. S corps provide an important option to be a corporation without the double tax, but let's examine the exact features below.

Pros

A very important pro is being pass-through. What does this really mean for you? When your business makes a profit, you will pay only one level of tax on that profit on your personal tax return filing. Whether you leave the money *in the business*, in other words, reinvest it into the business, you will still have to pay tax on that money that year.

If, in the beginning, if you spend more than you make, a pass-through entity will benefit you. You will be able to take the loss and reduce your taxable income. That's very cool, right? Well, running at a loss doesn't feel great, but at least you're saving on taxes!

Cons

Choosing to be an S corp is considered a privilege and there are some strict conditions you must meet. First, you must incorporate in the United States and be a tax resident of the United States. So must all the shareholders be.

An S corp cannot have more than one hundred owners. With this entity, since it's a pass-through, you pay tax regardless of whether you took the money out of the corporation. You may want to consider distributing some funds so that all shareholders can pay your taxes personally when the company is making money.

S corp shareholders can only be individuals (people like you and me), estates, and trusts. Despite this restriction, the S corp itself *may* own other entities, so the restriction only works in one direction in this case. Having your S corp own another entity could result in a best-of-both-worlds situation.

Finally, your S corp cannot have more than one class of stock. This means you can only have common stock without differentiating treatment. A lot of technical words, I know—here is an example of what it can look like. Remember I said Aviad and Ohad's showroom was an LLC taxed as an S corp? They split everything fifty-fifty: the money they put in, the money they take out. Imagine if they wanted to give Aviad 60 percent of the next round of distributions, and Ohad 40 percent. Doing that would immediately create a second class of stock in the eyes of the IRS and make the election to be an S corp invalid. The status would be lost and the entity would go "back" to a regular corporation (C corp) and the double taxation that comes with it.

Special note on LLCs taxed as S Corps

There is a way to "fix" the LLC if you already have one but have realized that it's not the best entity for you: you can file a form to become an S corp for *tax purposes only*. This election does *not* make a corporation out of you in the eyes of the Department of State; you are still a company. So, if you determined that having a corporation is great for you for other reasons, you may benefit from forming a brand-new entity.

There is always a reason behind a specific entity choice, and whether it's tax, liability protection, or both, keep in mind that it must ultimately address *your goals*, your vision, and your circumstances. This is a crucial step in your process, so feel free to pause before reading any further and jot down options that will work best for *you*.

8

Step Two: Determine Your Price Strategy

HAVE YOU EVER noticed how high-end restaurant prices are in whole dollars, and the price is matter-of-factly stated in small font below the dish description? It's almost like they want you to focus on how delicious that steak or fish is, so that your mouth waters just reading about sautéed something. You may be thinking that the menu layout is not a coincidence, and you are right: it's not. Restaurants are among the many companies that use price psychology techniques because they know how everyday consumers make purchasing decisions when it comes to price.

And if other businesses leverage the power of price, why wouldn't you? This chapter also applies if you've already launched. Let's take a look.

Pricing Strategy Options

There are two main pricing strategies to choose from: low-price leadership or high-value differentiation. Low-price leadership is certainly a strategy that can be perfected—just look at IKEA, Southwest Airlines, and Walmart. These companies built empires based on their commitment to low prices. Most low-price leadership companies, though, seem the same, don't you think? Words like "cheap" and "budget" come to mind when we think about these companies.

On the other hand, every high-value differentiation company appears to be different. They appeal to different consumers—regular people who value different features or benefits of the same product. High-value differentiation comes in many "flavors" because you can differentiate on a variety of bases. This strategy is about being different and focusing on value. Businesses often start because their owners don't like something about a product or an industry and are motivated to make something different. Warby Parker was started as a rebellion, for instance. The company's founders saw that the eyewear industry was dominated by a large company that kept prices for designer eyewear artificially high, and they decided to create an alternative. Don't confuse their strategy with low-price leadership; Warby Parker isn't trying to sell its glasses at the lowest possible price. It sells "higher quality, better-looking prescription eyewear at a fraction of the going price."[1]

Every category of product—and many categories of service—has a top-of-the-line brand. Take computers, for example. If you need a gaming or architectural drafting computer, you get a Windows-based computer, a PC. On the other hand, if you want a beautifully designed computer that's great for everyday work or home and is easy to use, you get an Apple computer.

Choosing a price strategy for your business idea is a critical step and I recommend that you do it now. Both options are certainly feasible, but I slightly favor high-value differentiation, when businesses compete on creating a value proposition for the customer and make themselves unique in some way.

Pretty much anything can be differentiated and value-driven, and if you haven't seen portable oxygen cans for sale or $5,000 car washes, check it out—do an internet search right now, in fact. Anything can be value-sold, a-n-y-t-h-i-n-g. It's all about the perceived value customers are getting in return for the money, and when that "value exchange" is in their favor, you will have a line of customers with their wallets out. Whatever price level you choose, pick one strategy now and stick to it.

Clear Value Proposition

When I went for my MBA, we spent a lot of time studying cases based on real companies. These cases were written by faculty at the Harvard Business School and were engaging, interesting, and often mind-blowing. One of the cases did strike me as unusual, to say the least: the case of Tesco, an originally British grocery chain, which has enjoyed tremendous success in Britain and around the world. Tesco was one of the first companies in its industry to adapt to the local cultures of markets it entered. For example, when Tesco opened up in Japan, it had to develop some product offerings—adding local food products and tweaking service, like adjusting its hours of operation. Tesco did this to make sure that the people of Japan embraced and accepted the Tesco brand, and it succeeded.

The pattern Tesco tested worked well in other countries; management listened to local communities and adapted the company to stand out. In the late 2000s, Tesco decided to penetrate and conquer the U.S. market with the same approach. Tesco strategically acquired existing supply chains, and, if you know anything about the U.S. grocery business, distribution is the number one challenge and a task to conquer.

Tesco seemed, according to the case materials our MBA class examined, to have offered various types of stores, from supermarkets to little groceries. Additionally, it emphasized ready-to-eat meals. Well, its U.S. adventure ended rather abruptly and it had to sell off all its operations, while financing the sale, just to curb losses.

Our marketing class examined the reasons for Tesco's failure in the United States. News outlets like CNBC theorized that it was all about bad timing,[2] but our marketing professor had a different theory. She thought that Tesco failed because it couldn't really define who it was and for whom. Tesco was a supermarket chain, a grocery store chain with ready meals at the same time, and small-city chain of shops. It acquired several different companies to penetrate the distribution network as well as existing smaller chains of various kinds. She stressed this lack of a cohesive identity in class and said numerous times in relation to other cases that it is important to clarify and define your mission: What is the one thing that you do, and who is the customer?

How can you avoid Tesco's mistake? Why are you starting this company? Why this business? What do you stand for? What are you offering your customers that's different from other companies? Take some time to develop your top-three value propositions. Complete the value proposition worksheet for *your* business idea (download this chart sample at dreamboldbook.com).

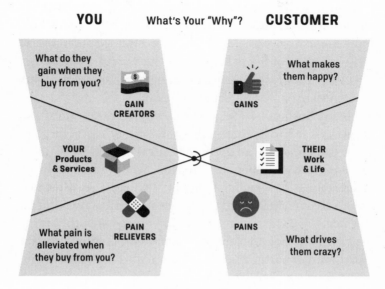

YOU   What's Your "Why"?   **CUSTOMER**

What do they gain when they buy from you?

GAIN CREATORS

GAINS

What makes them happy?

YOUR Products & Services

THEIR Work & Life

What pain is alleviated when they buy from you?

PAIN RELIEVERS

PAINS

What drives them crazy?

What Makes You Different?

Higher Prices Lead to Higher Profits

If you have a service, the recommended scenario is to create three levels of price-value options. For product-based businesses, creating three price options is a bit harder than for a service, and so you can benefit from using a what's called an upsell strategy. Upsell is often used when a customer is offered an accessory or an enhancement product when they select an expensive item. In his book *Price*, pricing expert Mark Wickersham explains why fees are a critical component of the profit equation. The profit equation is simple: *profit* equals s*ales* minus *expenses*. Sales are, then, the number of customers multiplied by the number of transactions per customer, multiplied again by the average customer order. Through his examples, Wickersham shows that a business pursuing a high-value differentiation strategy should raise prices, despite of risk of losing a few customers. Doing so will allow the business to create a better bottom line and less work and fewer expenses for your business.[3]

Many businesses focus on the top line (gross sales), so growing it at all costs becomes a new normal, a goal for aspiring entrepreneurs who don't know any better. New business owners often brag about their top line, while they are secretly losing money or spending their life's savings. They often find themselves trying to keep their business afloat, waiting for the next big payment or the next big client—or both. Let me be clear: it is not relevant to you or your potential investor, purchaser, or partner that you sell millions of dollars' worth of product or a service if, at the same time, you are losing money and cannot earn a profit. Focus on being profitable while growing sales—a much better way to impress all parties involved. Price is the tool to make that happen.

In this chapter I cover some of the pricing basics, but I don't go over every strategy—that would be a whole other book! However, you will have more than enough information to research a particular strategy and decide what's right for you. You can start by paying attention to how pioneers of industries price their products and services. Check out Apple's website and look at options presented for buying a computer. For example, before you add an iMac computer to your cart, you will be offered upgrades to the hard drive and memory and to purchase an additional keypad or headphones. Companies know that you're in buying mode and are purchasing a high-ticket item, so a lower-ticket item won't break your bank. How can you apply this strategy to your business offering? What are the "lower-ticket" accessories *you* can offer customers?

It isn't easy to position your business as a high-value brand when you're just starting out, but that doesn't mean you have to start at cheap—not at all. It means you have to up-level your company's communication of its value, and for *that* to happen, you have to know it and be clear about your value proposition. Refer back to the previous section if you need a refresher.

How Should You Price?

Whatever path you choose, low price or high value, pay attention to *how* you price. We will focus on high value because if you have chosen the low-price competition tactic, you will need to focus on always cutting costs to sustain your business.

When you focus on developing and building your value for services and certain products, such as software, create three levels of service—in other words, three packages. You want to capture price- and value-sensitive customers at the same time, as opposed to having just one offering for one type of client. Different people will always be willing to pay different prices, so you want to create options, just not so many that you confuse your customers.

The three options

The technique of offering different levels of access to your product or service is called price discrimination. It's effective in selling to more people by creating a range of prices for your offering and capturing consumers with varying willingness to pay.[4] This way you can still sell to those who cannot afford to pay for all the perks but really want *your* brand.

Start with creating a basic, low-level package, an introduction to your brand and your company. This price point will be for the price-sensitive customers, and when you create this level's value, be sure to incorporate a healthy profit for yourself and be willing to do the work or sell that service. For my accounting practice, I initially set up the low tier to be a "tax preparation only" service, covering the once-a-year tax filing. I soon realized that I set myself up for failure. In making a low tier like that, I created a potentially disastrous tax season for me and my team. Because all businesses and firms have to file taxes at the same time, we would end up working crazy hours during tax season and would not have time to provide ongoing advisory service to higher-paying clients. That didn't work for my firm, so I stopped offering that service completely.

Your top tier should be like an all-inclusive resort: the customer gets e-v-e-r-y-t-h-i-n-g. This tier should be priced really high: customers in this category will expect a luxury experience, so make sure that you are giving them exactly *that*, plus a nice cushion for you to make yourself or your resources available for those high-end clients on demand.

The middle package is where most people will "live," because, statistically, many gravitate toward the "not the cheapest, but also not the most expensive" option, so you want to make sure that this option provides solid value while priced with your target profit in mind.

It may take you some time to get your price right, but I want to caution you: Don't start low, start "somewhere in the middle." When I started my own tax practice, I often charged very little. I needed to grow so I took on every client that came in the door. This approach produced an unintended result within two years: as I built my reputation, produced tax-saving and tax compliance results for clients, I ended up with a large base of clients, many of whom felt that paying those very low fees entitled them to undivided, anytime attention to every "quick question" they had. So, instead of being able to focus on high-paying clients, who actually pay for my time and expertise, I ended up servicing everyone at the expense of family time. Does this seem fair? Well, yes, since I am the one to blame, but it's not fair to the higher-paying clients, or to me and my family, don't you think?

Don't make the same mistake I made. For your middle package, include a lot of value but not unlimited everything—set limits. Price it at a point that will make you feel fairly compensated and will yield a nice profit for your business.

Speaking of "nice profit," a common myth suggests that 30 percent is a good profit and should be your target. Don't go for that! You are not average, you are not everyone. You are *you* and anything is possible for your business. There are *no limits*. Are there companies with a 50 percent net profit? Heck, yes! Are there those that barely make 5 percent net? Absolutely. Don't set yourself up for failure by benchmarking your numbers to others. Apple doesn't do it and neither should you.

Positioning packages

Whenever you present your tiers and packages on your site or on a flyer, start with the most expensive service on the left side of the screen, then the middle option with a "best value" tag, and the cheapest on the right. Most of the world reads from left to right, and studies have shown that most people are loss averse, which means that when you take something away (like benefits they get in a package) it feels worse than when you add features in. People don't like to miss out on things, so presenting the choices in this "decreasing" manner will allow them to choose the best value they can afford, as opposed to just choosing simply based on price. For the software and the service industry, this approach makes a lot of sense and will pay off.

For the product industry, it may be challenging to present the packages as top to bottom, so you may want to get creative, like Apple. Interestingly, Apple does not list its options in the manner described, but even if you select a lower computer system package (less memory, less powerful hard drive, fewer screen inches), you are then offered to upgrade the memory, the hard drive, and the screen as part of the upselling process I mentioned earlier in this chapter.

When I switched to value pricing at my firm, I stopped billing on an hourly basis and developed packages that deliver value to clients. As a result, I had to change my routine with prospective clients. When holding a discovery call or a meeting, I focus on my top package first, because that's where my firm provides the most value and overarching support to you as a business owner. At this tier, I work with clients regularly and review their numbers, create plans and strategies, discuss and scrutinize potential financial decisions and their overall business direction, and handle tax strategy and planning.

OPTION	ELITE PACKAGE	VALUE PACKAGE	BASIC PACKAGE
Basic Benefit	✓	✓	✓
Basic Benefit	✓	✓	✓
Basic Benefit	✓	✓	✓
Basic Benefit	✓	✓	✓
Value Benefit	✓	✓	✗
Value Benefit	✓	✓	✗
Value Benefit	✓	✓	✗
Value Benefit	✓	✓	✗
Elite Benefit	✓	✗	✗
Elite Benefit	✓	✗	✗
Elite Benefit	✓	✗	✗
Elite Benefit	✓	✗	✗

In this support tier, my team and I are their back office and clients find it very valuable. It's also fairly expensive, so sometimes new clients cannot afford that level yet. If, upon reviewing their data, I determine that there is potential to get to that level in the near future, I offer that they can start at a lower package for six months as I guide them and help them grow, and, eventually, they can become an elite-level client.

How can you apply this strategy to your business? What tier would you prefer people to buy and you to service? Use the worksheet on page 116 (download it at dreamboldbook.com) to brainstorm your pricing packages.

The importance of decoys

A decoy is a technique in price psychology that can help you sell more of your preferred option. Dan Ariely, a well-known speaker and author of *Predictably Irrational*, once stumbled upon *The Economist* magazine's offering and couldn't believe his eyes.[5] Check it out—the options were as follows:

Web subscription $59
Print edition only $125
Print and web subscription $125

He was stunned because it wasn't clear why the magazine would even make the middle option available. Ariely later conducted a study with a large number of students and offered them the same options. He theorized that people see everything in relative terms, and he was right.

When presented with the three options above, 16 percent of students chose the "internet only" subscription, while 84 percent chose both print and web.[6] Nobody chose the middle option. In his next round, he removed the middle "print only" option. The new results were a bit shocking: 68 percent chose internet only (the cheaper option), while 32 percent chose print and web.

So, if you are *The Economist*, in the first scenario, if you were to sell one thousand subscriptions, you would have made:

$1{,}000 \times 16\% \times \$59 = \$9{,}440$
plus
$1{,}000 \times 84\% \times \$125 = \$105{,}000$
for a total of $114,440.

On the other hand, the second scenario without that decoy in the middle would yield:

$1{,}000 \times 32\% \times \$59 = \$18{,}880$
plus
$1{,}000 \times 68\% \times \$125 = \$85{,}000$
for a total of $103,880.

The difference between the two options on only one thousand subscriptions is a whopping $10,560 or 10.17 percent. Imagine the effect on the bottom line if the magazine sold one hundred thousand subscriptions instead of just a thousand. In fact, in 2011, it had more than three million digital and one hundred thousand print subscribers, to put things in perspective.

You may not be able to use a decoy in every situation, but knowing that this technique exists is pretty empowering, so take notice. Now, let's look at anchors.

Anchors

A powerful related technique is to create high-priced anchors in customers' minds. A price anchor is so effective that millions of brands use this technique every year to make prices of their other products seem small.[7] Think about a store like Marshalls. Its tags always have the "original" or "compare to" price, which is almost always much higher than what you are paying for the item. Especially when they sell popular clothing brands that are generally expensive, the store makes sure you see that an item previously cost *a lot more* than what you are paying for it today. Even stores like Marshalls have ultra-high-ticket items, so if you don't want to fall into the anchor trap, disregard the "compare to" or "previously at" price on the ticket. Rather, decide about the item in your hand solely on the current price-value balance.

A well-known case of a Williams Sonoma bread maker proved just how powerful an anchor can be.[8] The store's most expensive item in line was close to $300 and wasn't selling very well. Then Williams Sonoma introduced a top-of-the-line model selling for more than $400, and suddenly the other one flew off the shelves. Why do you think this happened? It seems that compared with the new and more expensive one, this lower-priced-but-still-expensive bread maker suddenly looked less expensive.

Don't underestimate the power of an anchor. Famous jewelry brands create one-of-a-kind items that are prominently displayed in stores or online at astronomical prices. Those items are prominently displayed to make you feel like the price you see for another product is a bargain. Remember this when you price your next product or service and create your pricing strategy. Can you create a one-of-a-kind anchor for what you do or make?

Other pricing techniques

There are other techniques you can employ in your pricing, and all can be important. You want to get the maximum price customers are willing to pay, while making sure that you can generate a healthy profit to support your business and your vision.

Generally, the smaller the number is visually, the smaller it seems to our brain, so we can justify the purchase more easily. Also, the fewer the digits, the lower the price seems. So, if you are opening a restaurant, don't make customers focus on the price by adding ".99"—it is distracting and not at all helpful for selecting a meal. Recall that fine dining restaurants always make the price small, almost unnoticeable, so that you focus on the dish. Smart, right? Use it!

On the other hand, for department stores and other product-based businesses that compete on price, the "left digit" (for example, the "2" in the price "$299" or "$99" instead of "$100") is more important: although the price is less by only a dollar or a penny, because the left digit is smaller, our brains think the price is lower! No wonder larger companies have long used this effectively. Frankly, it works very well on me, as it is so much easier to tell my husband that something was "$300" when it cost $399. In my mind it's three hundred and change, even though I know it's *really* four hundred!

Let's take a look at ending your price with a zero, a seven, or a nine. When a price ends in zero, it may seem higher, or even "made up." A price ending in zero is probably ideal for your most basic package, because you want to sell more of the higher-priced items rather than the basic, cheapest option, don't you? A price ending in seven, on the other hand, makes it more difficult for customers to do the math in their heads, if it's a monthly or a per quantity rate, or when you break down the total price into several chunks. It's easy to say, "Well, $99 a month is roughly $100, so $1,200 per year"; but when the "right digit" is further reduced to seven, interestingly, many people don't round that calculation up to $100 in their heads.

Instead, they often look only at that monthly amount. This can make seven a better ending for the package you *do* want to sell most.

To get your price right, though, you need to test different things, so a trial-and-error approach here is critical. Selecting your initial strategy early on is important because it will determine how you approach your pricing in the long run. You will find that it is often more about testing different approaches and analyzing your test results than it is about a one-and-done technique. Even if you've been in business for a while, review your prices at least every six months—or even more frequently, depending on your business type. You will find that your costs increase regularly for the products and service you use in your business, so it's only natural to raise prices every so often to make sure your bottom line is still solid.

Sometimes, you may find yourself in an unfamiliar territory and will need a complex, multilevel pricing structure and testing that goes beyond your own knowledge. You will want to be strategic with price increases and price structure redesigns, because you wouldn't want to do something and watch your customers leave you, right? Sometimes, you will want to hire a pricing expert, someone who has the experience and the ability to calculate predicted customer loss with every price increase—someone who will help you do this better and with less risk to your business.

Price psychology is a tool that can transform your bottom line, no question. But there is something even more powerful: managing your cash can transform your entire business and life. Let's look at that next.

9

Step Three: Set Up Your "Cash Is King" Routine

"OH MY GOSH, I don't know what to do," Sandra said. She looked upset as I saw her on my screen. It was our first call and we were going over what services she was looking for. "My business brings in close to $1 million a year and yet every two weeks I struggle to make payroll and only take a thousand for myself. This is so frustrating."

"You've got to get your cash flow under control," I said. "There are quite a few things you can do. Let's start with your weekly routine."

Conversations like these happen nearly every week in my office. Sometimes I feel like business owners look at one another and get the impression that everyone else has cash under control, and *they* are the only ones struggling with it so much.

Although it's slightly cliché, cash is definitely king, especially when you are just starting out and cannot afford to waste any. For all kinds of start-up ventures, cash management is critical, and that's why we are talking about it in this chapter. Don't worry: it's not rocket science. You will feel like it's a pain in the beginning and may even want to quit, but *don't*. This step is *so critical* that if you get only one thing out of this book, this should be it. You will see the effects and the value of cash planning as soon as you are through your first month in business. I guarantee it.

Do you find yourself wondering what "cash management" really means? Everyone talks about it, but do you know what it means for you and your business idea? Simply put, managing cash is how you spend your resources and whether you can make your immediate bill payments with the cash on hand. It also means that you know ahead of time when you are going to be tight with cash and when you will have an abundance of it. Knowing those cash "dips" ahead of time will enable you to plan for them by stretching a payable or two, or by offering a customer a discount to speed up collections. Knowledge will give you confidence in your numbers and will help you stick to your budget. You will be able to have your business "diagnosis" at your fingertips and tell whether or not you can afford to hire an additional staff member and investigate your over- and under-spends.

If you try to wing it by simply looking at your bank balance, which is what even many seasoned entrepreneurs and business owners do, you will fall into a trap. Your decisions will send you spiraling down into debt in your "down" months and it could potentially snowball into something more serious. In his book *Profit First*, Mike Michalowicz calls it "the survival trap."[1] A survival trap happens when we are caught up in that mode of waiting for the "next big customer," the "next big payment," or the next big hurdle we conquer for relief from the constant cash strain, and it never happens. The struggle continues indefinitely until you do something about it. Since you are reading this book now, you have a pretty good chance of avoiding this trap.

Many businesses run out of cash simply because cash management is put on the back burner. Don't be one of them! As the old saying goes, "Learn from the mistakes of others... You can't live long enough to make them all yourself!"

But although you can leave it to others to make the mistakes, you can't delegate your own cash management to someone else—at least not yet. And even when you can delegate, you will have your own strategy and will always need to stay on top of it. So, plan for cash inflows and outflows; keep a tight grip on cash and it will help you get to your goal with fewer mistakes. Get used to the fact that you will have to learn, know, and own your numbers. You will, at times, feel scared and concerned about your numbers not being what you have projected, so you may be tempted to just look away and avoid stress. It's a trap. Don't do it. Face them instead: make numbers the cornerstone of your business and life. Doing so will empower you to evaluate and act deliberately in times of crisis. You will decide quickly to either salvage a stalled situation or ride the momentum you've got.

Get Your Spreadsheets Out

We first met David and his company Nasty Pig in chapter 4. David has become a phenomenal CEO by learning his numbers and developing his own management tools. He is now a master of cash management. David, with the help of advisors (myself included), used Excel to develop a simple cash flow forecast, which outlined every item of income and expense for the next twelve months. This model allowed David to *look into the future*, so to speak. But to get it running, David first had to look at the past several years of revenue to help him estimate. He created a spreadsheet, where he tracked monthly sales by channel (in-store, online, wholesale, and trade show). After that, David assumed a few ways his sales could grow, conservatively, and ran a percent increase or decrease calculation on a monthly and annual basis, then did an average increase or decrease month to month and, finally, predicted monthly cash collections for the next year. That determined how much cash he projected to bring in every month.

David's next step was planning for expenses. For anyone except accountants, this is a tough one. It's painful because it should be done line by line. There is no other way to really learn your numbers. And doing it will make you a freaking awesome CEO. So, accept it and get to it. When we worked on the first cash flow forecast together, we started with things he knew were more or less predetermined: production team salaries, store staff salaries, rent, phone bill, utilities, and trade show travel costs. Lastly, at the bottom of the cash flow forecast we listed monthly payments for loans and credit cards. That allowed him to plan for cash outflows that don't usually appear on a profit and loss statement.

At the end of this exercise, David could see where he would be each month, cash-wise. He could also plan to use excess cash to fund future months, when cash would be tight. Or he could plan an expansion and be sure that he could afford it. It was empowering for David to see if he could afford to hire a staff member or ramp up his marketing efforts.

On pages 128–29 is a sample of a cash flow forecast you can use. Download this tool in a spreadsheet format by going to dreamboldbook.com. Spend some time with it. Start with a few details off the top of your head, like rent, employee salaries, software. Let it marinate in your brain for a few days—don't rush. I cannot stress enough the importance of running your numbers before you go any further. When you are done, you'll know whether or not you can afford to start now or will need a money boost. If you skip this step, you're running a risk of losing money you cannot afford to lose. Start with expenses instead of income and go line by line estimating how much will you realistically need to pay for your major expenses. A good start is to plan the first ninety days, or roughly three months, of your operations once you open. You may need to do some research on expenses customary for your industry and type of service. A simple internet search is a good start for that.

My client Scott and his partners had a small print shop in New York. Another business they owned did large print installations around the country (think billboards and bus wraps). Business was good and the company wanted to grow. An opportunity to buy a failing print shop in a great location and with a solid customer list presented itself and Scott asked me to help him understand whether the purchase was a good deal for them. I applied the same method described here. Scott and I spent several days polishing the numbers, creating three scenarios considering all potential costs, debts, and sales needed to make it work. Scott really wanted this deal, but I kept pushing back for numbers. Creating those cash scenarios was brutal for both of us. It was a painful brain exercise. In the end, Scott and I determined that even with a best-case scenario, the company would need a cash infusion of at least a half a million dollars in year one. This was a "no-go" and we walked away from this deal. Scott and his partners have thanked me many times since then for doing my job and keeping my eyes on cash.

The table below shows a sample spreadsheet for how you would approach your cash flow forecast. Once you're confident in your expenses, record sales numbers. Do not just focus on "paper sales": think about how much *cash* you can realistically bring in. Expenses will always come due, but income is not yet guaranteed, so examine your income assumptions. Are they valid? Do you know your audience well? Will they buy from you when you think they will?

Income	Month 1
A-Service Package 1	$10,000
A-Service Package 2	$7,500
And/or	
B-Product Series 1	$20,000
B-Product Series 2	0
Total Income/Cash Inflow	**$37,500**

Cost of Sales (aka Variable Costs)	
A- and/or B-direct staff costs	$3,000
B-direct material cost	$7,500
A- and/or B-other direct costs (commissions, shipping)	$750
Total Cost Outflow	**$11,250**
Gross Profit[1]	**$26,250**

Expenses	Month 1
Marketing and promo	$1,000
Non-production staff	$6,000
Travel	$1,500
Officer compensation (your pay)[2]	$10,000
General/admin expenses (office supplies, software, rent, utilities)	$2,500
Professional fees	$1,250
Taxes and licenses[3]	$500
Other items	$300
Total Expenses	**$23,050**
Net Income[4]	**$3,200**

Cash: Beginning of Month[5]	**$0**
Cash: Ending of Month[6]	**$3,200**

1 Gross profit is your top-line income less cost of sales.

2 Officer compensation means *your* pay, or the owner's pay. How much do you need to have the lifestyle you want?

3 Taxes and licenses are generally entity-level income taxes, payroll taxes, and property taxes if that applies.

4 Net income is your bottom line.

5 Your cash at the beginning of your first month will be whatever cash you are investing and have available to spend. Every month after that, it will be the same as the cash at the end of the previous month.

6 Cash at the end of the month will be beginning cash plus net income for that month. If it's a loss for a month, the ending cash will decrease.

You don't have to spend as much time as Scott and I did on this exercise; after all, you are not buying a failing shop, nor are you combining companies with numerous partners and staff already on payroll, so this process will be a lot easier for you. Take a look at the sample on dreamboldbook.com, see what you can come up with, and talk to others to see if you are potentially missing something. If you need a bit of help, I run "work sprints" several times a week, where all attendees do their own work, their bookkeeping or planning, for twenty-five minutes, and then for whoever has questions, we do a Q&A session for five minutes, and then repeat.[2] Check out programs.tatianatsoir.com for dates and times and come get your questions answered.

David, Nasty Pig CEO, has always been a creative person, a visionary, and back in the day "numbers" were not his strong suit. He knew he needed to get them under control and by "just doing it" he learned to understand and use numbers to his advantage. Throughout economic downturns he "kept a tight ship" and made decisions after reviewing his twelve-month cash plan. David doesn't know everything about accounting and taxes, but he doesn't need to know *everything*. The same applies to you: you don't need to know it *all* when it comes to numbers, bookkeeping, and taxes—but you need to know enough to make smart and timely decisions for your business. Going through this exercise will eliminate the "what ifs" that come with starting and running a business. And as you are getting ready to do it, remember the famous saying: "How do you eat an elephant? One bite at a time!"

Working with David made me realize that new businesses often miss that critical piece of the puzzle: planning ahead. For whatever reason, it becomes a psychological burden, where it seems like it is almost better not to know what the future holds or that you are not good with numbers or another excuse. It's a trap! Don't fall for it. Plan your future and then make it happen.

The Importance of Taking Your Profit First

Profit First by Mike Michalowicz changed my client's business. James was running a small clothing brand company in New York City, and at a certain point he decided to invest a significant amount of cash into renovating his physical store. At about the same time, his newest collection didn't do as well as he had hoped. So, in September of that year, as he needed to pay a 30 percent deposit on the spring/summer collection for the following year, and pay the balance of 70 percent on the current year's fall collection that was starting to sell, James ran out of cash. He was terrified. He had to borrow more than $250,000 to make his production payments. He had a few loans on the books before that, so in about a year from that time his debt was up to about $1 million. Monthly payments alone were over $20,000. He knew that something had to change.

I started working with James about a year into this massive debt. It took me about six months to get acquainted with the business and its cycle and intricacies of overseas production. One evening, James called me and said, "Tatiana, I read *Profit First* and it's amazing! We are doing it, I set up the accounts already. From now on you will transfer 1 percent to each account every day." At the time I had never heard about this book, but I wanted to help my client. Before James implemented this new system, he had to borrow more money during every August/September cash dip and slowly pay it back.

If you have not heard of the Profit First method, you must check it out. It's a method that may make the difference between your business's survival and closing up shop. In the book, Michalowicz walks you through a system of working with your habits, rather than trying to change them. Business owners often manage their cash by looking at their bank balance and making decisions based on a balance that day. That's a habit of failure because you may miss payments coming up in the near future and spend money before that.

The Profit First system works by splitting your incoming cash into four main purpose "buckets": profit, taxes, your compensation, and operating expenses. You create a total of five main bank accounts: the ones just mentioned plus an income account to receive all your cash from customers. You then make systematic transfers from the income account to the other four and spend only the funds available in those accounts. For example, you pay yourself out of the "your compensation" bank account, while you do not touch what's in the profit and tax accounts until it's time to do so. The idea is that you take your profit first, quarterly, and learn to transform your business into a lean machine.

Although the Profit First system was meant to be used in existing businesses, you will be ahead of the game when you apply it to your business during this cash flow planning stage and set yourself up for profitability and predictability of your cash.

A year into applying this system for James's company, we stopped borrowing during the September cash crunch. Three years after that, his debt was down to about half a million dollars, and later it was paid off completely. You can get great results by starting out with this system and skip all the anxiety related to debt. I encourage you to check out *Profit First* by Mike Michalowicz as your next read.

Realistic Versus Ambitious Planning

You may feel like the detailed planning we just covered will take your eyes off your vision and, possibly, demotivate you. It won't, I promise. When I work with clients to help them get out of the rat race, I often suggest creating two plans. The first is a conservative and realistic plan for cash flow management, to understand and better manage expenses and know when to save ahead for larger expenses or to reinvest back in the business. The second plan is more ambitious, the plan that will encourage and motivate you to find creative ways to achieve the goals you set. You will want to have a big goal, but also keep a tight grip on your cash.

Once you launch, you will compare your forecasted amounts to the amounts actually spent regularly and investigate every discrepancy. Discrepancies are not bad; you just need to understand why they happened and prevent them from happening again. After you have done this for a few months, you will never have a doubt or a fear in your mind, and you will know where you are going and what return on investment you can expect. All it takes is a little time to plan and you'll be on your way.

Depending on how often you get cash in the bank from customers (monthly, weekly, daily), set up a routine to review your progress toward your cash flow goal. You will need to see trends and identify, the sooner the better, where you run under budget (income) and over budget (expenses) early so that you can course-correct. Some of my best clients review their numbers daily, watch their progress, spot unfavorable trends, and develop a plan of action to keep them on track, and so should you.

After week one of a given month, run a budget versus actuals report and observe your progress toward your monthly forecast. As for income, does your number equal to roughly a quarter of your monthly goal? There may be spikes in revenue if your business is cyclical, but you should consider that ahead of time and not be worried when you see that on the report. If you are worried because you are not where you should be, take it as your early call to action: find out why and do something about it! As far as expenses are concerned, if you see that in a given week you surpassed your budget for office meals, then maybe it's time to stop being overly generous and reschedule a few "great but unnecessary" meetings for the following month, when the budget will reset. (But it will still be there!)

Revisit your aspirational goals quarterly. You can see where you are and how you are progressing to the most ambitious goals you've ever had. The key in keeping control of cash is *planning* and monitoring, so put those tasks on your daily to-do list even before you launch. When I ask clients to create these goals, they get inspired and driven by limitless possibilities that are there for them to explore. There really is no limit to what you can do when you set out to do it.

10

Step Four:
Get Your Tax Strategy

TAXES FREAK EVERYONE OUT. We genuinely dislike having to do them and having to pay someone to do them; we despise paying taxes and even thinking about them. And the feeling is the same across the board. Even accountants often wait until the last minute to file their *own* taxes. The only time we like anything tax-related is when we get to save on taxes, and that's what makes us all excited—of course!

A few years ago I got an email from the Internal Revenue Service professionals email list with the subject line: "Taxpayers' Bill of Rights No. 3: The Right to Pay No More Than the Correct Amount of Tax." This, in plain English, means that it is *your right* to use the tax law provisions and its benefits to pay *as little as legally possible* to the government. Especially if you have a business, there are numerous tax strategies out there for you: income shifting, entity restructuring, hidden business deductions, and deferrals, just to name a few. Despite that the final determination of whether certain things you pay for become a tax deduction is done by your accountant, they usually won't know what you spend unless you give them more details and argue that something is a business expense.

Remember the back-office myths in chapter 1, where we talked about how, even if you are just starting out and aren't making money yet, you have to still address your bookkeeping and taxes? Filing will provide for some important tax benefits either immediately or in the near future or both. You don't need to know or understand everything about taxes, but since you are starting a business, knowing some basics will help you pay less of them.

Separating Business from Personal

Your business money should always be separate from your personal money.

Do people mix business and personal income and expenses? All the time, but it's not a good idea. I often find people surprised at this simple truth: when you keep business and personal income and expenses separately, it's always easier to go through an audit, if it ever happens. When you pay personal expenses out of the business account, if you get audited (which is not as scary as it seems), it will be harder to prove the business purpose of expenses that *could* be deemed both personal and business.

This separation doesn't mean that to test-drive your idea you have to form a legal entity. It just means that when you accept payments from customers and pay for business expenses, you should use bank accounts and credit cards that don't have any personal items going through them. If you occasionally use the wrong card, just reimburse the correct account by transferring the same amount of funds back into the wrongly charged account. When it comes to credit cards, especially in the beginning, you *may* use cards under your personal name for business, but if you are doing so, keep those designated cards for business only.

Finally, if you have several expenses that are mostly personal but also used for business, such as a car and a home office, I recommend paying them out of your personal account, or possibly even one separate account, so that you can easily tally it at year-end.

Car expenses will include gas, insurance, maintenance and repairs, DMV fees, parking, and tolls. Do keep those last ones, parking and tolls, on a business card. They are a separate deduction and are fully deductible if they are related to business.

Home office expenses include home insurance, mortgage interest, real estate taxes, or rent, condo charges, utilities, internet service, landscaping, and waste management. Pay all these from a designated personal account, total it up and take a portion of it as a business expense for your taxes when you file. If you own your home and run your business out of it, I recommend hiring an experienced accountant to deal with home office deductions, as there are a few options and wrinkles.

Good Questions!

I had a twenty-minute introductory call with a potential client. Andrew and his partner had just started a micro-gym. They launched a week prior to the call and wanted to hire an accountant-advisor. The questions Andrew and his partner asked are very common, so you may have the same ones. Let's review three of them.

Question 1: Do we need to file taxes even if we didn't make any money?

The answer is yes, because in your first year you may not make any profit and may even lose money, but losses provide a very important tax benefit, so it always pays to file taxes. Moreover, if you have already organized the entity (created an LLC or a corporation), the government will look for that filing, so make sure you file.

Question 2: Do you offer a more start-up-friendly package?

I mentioned to Andrew that I was not currently working with businesses that are just starting out because they usually have a tight budget and my fees are high. That's the reason I wrote this book: to make my expertise and knowledge accessible to more people who cannot afford to hire someone like me, and, at the same time, cannot afford *not* to. I told Andrew that investing in this book, reading it, and implementing its basics will ensure that he has the money to hire a great accountant at the exact moment he must, because he will have saved enough money by handling all the back-office fundamentals right from the start.

Question 3: What's your opinion on Profit First's Target Allocation Percentages?

Every start-up is different. What is good for your friend's business may not work for yours. I am a huge fan of Profit First and subscribe to it 100 percent, and I feel Profit First Professionals are out there for a reason. You could definitely implement the system on your own, but a professional will help you adapt this system to *your* business. The same applies when you are just starting out: you should do some research, look at other businesses if you are able to, and remember to be lean. It is your job—and your highest priority—to run lean. You are the one who will talk to your landlord to negotiate the lease, speak to your factories to negotiate the timing of deposits you need to pay for a collection, or talk to your vendors to adjust their payment schedule to a certain day of the month. Some businesses don't need their operating expenses to be at a certain percent if they can manage with less. Remember, any great system only gives you guidelines; you have to own them and apply them to your business, either yourself or with the help of a business advisor.

Reporting Your Income

Income is fairly simple. Any time money comes to your designated business account, you should show it as income, unless it is clearly not because it's a transfer from your personal account or from different bank accounts in the same business (a simple transfer). Whenever you receive a refund of an insurance premium, for example, list it as "other income" instead of offsetting the same expense; it will be easier to make sense of it if there is ever an audit.

Then, keep track of your capital infusions and also money you take out for personal expenses. You may be tempted to pay personal expenses directly from a business account. Don't. Instead, transfer money from your designated business account to a purely personal account and pay personal expenses out of that. Doing so will ensure that your year-end tracking becomes a thirty-minute job, while you can sleep well at night knowing that you have all the backups and can withstand an audit.

Income Shifting Mindset

My client Mark is a divorced man with two grown children and a girlfriend. He helps all of them financially as much as he can. One of his daughters is a teacher and the other is an event planner, both at the start of their careers. Every year Mark gives his kids money to help out with rent, student loans, and things like getting a car, if they need it. His girlfriend needed help overcoming a financial hurdle and Mark gave her money regularly, as well. Before starting to work with my firm, Mark just transferred "after tax" money to support his loved ones—in other words, what he had left after he filed and paid his taxes, which means money for which he did not get a tax deduction.

After Mark and I started working together, my firm and I did a complete review and analysis of Mark's business and personal dealings and determined that all of those seemingly personal payments could have yielded a valuable tax benefit: a deduction.

For example, if you are supporting an adult child or a relative, have them help you out and handle a few tasks so that you can pay them out of your business. Young adults tend to handle social media well, and older generations may be well-suited to admin tasks, so if they provide you service, pay them out of your business. Pay them more to cover taxes but get yourself that deduction! Do get your ducks in a row with proper insurance and employment contracts in place and comply with minimum wage laws.

Over a period of a few months, Mark shared with me that he no longer wanted to make any money moves without checking with my firm first, and I cannot blame him. Remember: after you have already paid someone, it's too late to go back and change it, so think *before* you pay. As for Mark, his payments amounted to more than $50,000 per year, which, at a 40 percent tax rate, could have saved him about $20,000. Do you think it's worth implementing income shifting strategies for this money? I do! Set your mind for saving tax money, and get your backup in order at the same time.

Understanding What's Deductible

Given that this book is not providing legal or tax advice, I will not tell you whether something you've paid for is deductible or not, but I will show you examples of what can be an ordinary and necessary business expense per IRS regulations.

Generally, a business expense is anything that a reasonable businessperson would deem ordinary and necessary in the normal course of doing business. These will differ for nearly every business, and it makes sense. For example, buying makeup and paying for hair styling wouldn't be a necessary expense for an accountant, but it would be for a professional dancer or performer. Similarly, buying luxury clothing is not an expense you would typically see for an attorney, but buying them from your retailer as a quality control mechanism for a clothing brand could be acceptable.

You will typically have some direct costs that should come right after gross revenue, such as direct labor, direct materials, and the cost of the product you are selling. Those are considered *variable costs*, but to help you get this concept, think of it this way: if you weren't producing any products or services, these costs would be zero. These costs should be presented differently on your reports and on your tax filings.

Many businesses have some of the typical overhead expenses, such as office or workspace rent, utilities (water, electric, oil, or gas), telephone, office supplies, staff salaries and related taxes, computers and software, subscriptions, professional fees (attorneys, accountants, IT, designers, and so on), travel, and advertising. Those are known as *fixed costs*, and would still have to be paid even if you made no sales. The list of expenses is not exhaustive, but I do want to caution you regarding personal expenses. If the true reason you are buying something is that you are making it look like it's for business, then it's better just claim it as a personal—and therefore nondeductible—expense. A new phone, for example, that you will also use for personal matters, would be a personal expense, but if your main source of client calls and business is via that phone, then it may be a deductible business expense.

There are certain limits on expenses such as meals, entertainment, car lease, and car-related expenses. We discussed car expenses earlier, but be aware that you should keep a log of business versus personal trips as proof. There are phone apps that can do that easily for you, you'd just need to log in and designate each trip, which you can do weekly or daily.

The goal of this section is to build a habit in you, so that every time you are at a store register or at a restaurant table, you think whether this expense is a business or a personal one and pull the appropriate card out and set up a routine of doing a few painful-but-necessary tasks regularly.

Hidden Deductions and Write-Offs

Back in the day when I actively networked, I belonged to a group of divorce professionals in the area. It was a national organization's chapter in New York. As part of the membership, I was scheduled to present an educational talk on a specific topic and I chose "divorce and taxes." I talked about what's important in a divorce from a tax perspective: doing the divorce agreement with taxes in mind, making sure that any pension account transfers are done with the correct court order to avoid penalties, and handling the custody and tax exemptions fairly, just to name a few. I also talked about common omissions and missed tax-saving opportunities that most traditional preparers overlook because they lack time to pay enough attention to every tax return they process during tax season. I mentioned that, if certain conditions are met, wine, health club, and certain hobby and personal expenses *could* be deductions, some of which surprised the group.

It is helpful to consider everything you spend, so keeping good records is very important, but it doesn't have to be expensive or hard or otherwise very involved. For my household's finances I use Intuit's QuickBooks Online. It has a very powerful banking engine, works with almost every bank, and makes handling it easy. All relevant family members can access it and look at reports. Our family has a number of bank and credit card accounts for various purposes (club memberships, mile benefits, and cash backs), and they are all connected through QuickBooks Online. To get a head start, you can use its cheapest version, because it's inexpensive and gets you to your goal of tracking expenses. With over thirty accounts, it takes me fifteen minutes every month to update all activities and categorize all our spending for that month. After that time spent, I know exactly how much we spend on gas, home maintenance, groceries, and insurance. I can then take a portion of expenses for a home office and deduct them as a business expense and reduce my tax due.

You may know ballpark numbers of what you spend and may think that having a system is a waste of time. You may be right, but the Internal Revenue Service doesn't particularly like estimates, and calendar year cutoff dates are important for taking deductions. Here is what I mean. Usually, school tax is broken into several installments to make it easier for households to manage. One installment can be due, say, in September, while another will be due in December or January. So, when you are gathering your numbers for taxes, you may count your "annual commitment" school tax number, but if you made that second payment in January, you are not allowed to count it in as a deduction until the following year. In plain English: neither an approximate nor a tentatively paid item will provide you a legal tax benefit if you cannot prove it was paid when you say it was paid. Keeping an expense tracking system will also help your tax planner develop processes to pay the least amount of tax legally.

Lastly, keep a good paper and money trail for all deductions you claim. Proving that you rented a part of your large home to your spouse for their office is much harder if there is no lease or regular rent payments in place. It could be considered a "sham" transaction and disregarded completely. It can really screw up your prior tax returns and cause you a lot of anxiety, so prevent this from happening by paying attention to detail and getting your ducks in a row.

Look for the Uncommon Approach

Brandon came to my firm very recently as an introduction from an existing client. A successful realtor, he built up a team of agents under his umbrella, ran virtual tours, filmed property introductions, and ran a podcast. His entity was a one-person LLC, and the previous year he made more than $300,000 in net profit. Brandon wanted to keep investing in real estate himself, and his goal was to own and rent out a number of properties. With his level of income, it could make sense to create a multi-entity structure and shift income legally between them. One entity could operate as a mortgage lender to Brandon, who would then purchase and manage several real estate properties. Given that Brandon already qualified as a real estate professional for tax purposes, his potential tax savings were limitless!

What does Brandon's case have to do with you? It's an illustration of an uncommon approach to servicing a real estate professional. Usually, traditional accounting firms don't do this kind of planning and strategizing: there simply isn't enough time for it. Brandon's case is just one example of how every client is different and is here to illustrate an out-of-the-box approach you should look for in your professional.

After you've read this chapter, you should always approach every expense with the same question: is there a tax deduction for *that*? You will also be compelled to look for a tax advisor who will help you learn more and structure your business in such a way as to allow you to pay less taxes, yet incorporate only reasonable and legitimate strategies. In appendix 3 of this book, I talk about what a great advisor looks like, how you find one, and what questions you should ask.

One important factor to consider as you do tax planning is the possibility of an audit. Many clients have told me that just thinking about an audit causes them anxiety. It doesn't help that the process of an audit is full of mystery; it's random yet extensive. But you shouldn't be afraid of an audit.

My client Mark told me that right before we started working together he went through an IRS audit. He said that going through it was scary at first, as he had never been audited before. As the process unfolded, it turned out to be "not that bad." He had to pull a lot of bills, statements, and receipts from his archives for the year under audit (which is usually two to three years in the past), so it just took a little time. He later received a "no-change" letter, which is the perfect outcome everyone wants. But to get that result, you've got to keep good records—this is a must. Then you can skip the anxiety and always be prepared to prove your deductions.

11

Step Five: Know When to Seek Help

N O MATTER HOW hard we try to push forward, no matter how tough and resilient we want to seem, all of us sometimes need a fresh set of eyes in the form of support and guidance so we don't lose the forest for the trees. In this chapter I talk about outside help—the kind you pay for. Help from attorneys, coaches, and accountants. This does not mean to say you can't do it all yourself. You can... but if you want to grow, scale, and eventually get the freedom you imagined for yourself, you will need to get help at various milestones of your business idea development and throughout your business growth.

Sometimes we are sold something we don't need *right now*. Since you can't make a mistake and waste money, how do you know when to go out on a limb financially and hire an attorney, a coach, or an accountant for our business idea? Getting the right help at the right time doesn't mean you're weak. Just the opposite—and it can provide a boost to take you to the next milestone faster. Let's look at these helpers one by one.

Attorneys

In the beginning stages of a business launch, attorneys can be important in several scenarios. Attorneys specialize in different areas of law and you may need one at various stages of your growth—but you may also not need one for a while.

A start-up attorney

If you are a tech start-up and your goal is to raise serious funding and sell your idea and company, then you will need a start-up attorney who specializes in legal matters of protecting you and setting up the legal foundation. My client Frank got lucky back in 2012, when one of the largest and most well-known start-up law firms had a program that offered free legal service. They not only handled reorganization filings but also advised on various instruments that potential investors would like to see. Moreover, they prepared and filed Frank's patent applications, and all of that was free! Otherwise, services of that caliber of firm would have cost tens of thousands of dollars, which you'd need to pay out of pocket.

Remember, when you know you are seeking a significant-sized investor, you can always hire a high-caliber start-up attorney, because they can have an pool of investors and can share insights into what those investors need to see in *your* start-up so that you have a better chance of securing capital from them. Otherwise, save money and get your basics done by a pro for an affordable amount.

An intellectual property attorney

You may need an intellectual property attorney if you have a proprietary product or a process, and their services are far from cheap. Be mindful that intellectual property filings aren't always required right away. In many cases, you can file a preliminary application to secure a spot in line first. You will then have a period of time to submit the filing, which is the expensive part. Don't rush into it right away. You may not even need or want it. Consider that Coca-Cola hasn't patented its formula; the company just keeps it a secret.

Remember, and this goes for all professionals, that the work is their bread and butter. I have seen attorneys encourage clients to file when they could have waited, and I've seen attorneys recommend start-ups purchase errors and omissions insurance before they really needed to use it. So, remember that the choices are ultimately up to you. Make sure *you* know why you need something done *right now*—or whether it can wait.

A business and securities attorney

If you're not a tech start-up and are just starting out, you can find a business and securities lawyer.[1] But I'm not sure you need to spend money on that at the very beginning. There are companies that specialize in organizing entities and can do the basics well. These companies can get state approvals, file incorporation documents for you, get a tax ID for your business, perform lien searches, and do up boilerplate documents, all for a reasonable fee.

If you are opening up a franchised business or are using retirement money to fund your venture, you may need a specialty lawyer to make sure that what you are signing is fair to you. As soon as you sign something freely, you are stuck with it and have obligations and liabilities under that document. Pay close attention and read anything you sign. Frank, whom you may recall that I met through my client Michael, shared that Michael taught him the "secret to reading contracts." I got curious as to what the secret was. And the secret to reading contracts is... *to actually read the contracts.* Shocking, right? You must read and understand what you are getting into, or you need to pay an attorney to do so. Protecting your interests is your obligation.

Remember the few scenarios in which you may want to have a strategic partner? Well, if that's the route you chose, be sure to have a good agreement in place—for better or for worse. Do not rely on well-known legal-aid websites and a standard agreement. *Get your own.* To save money, you *may* start with a standard agreement and have your attorney edit it for clauses that are important to *you*. This approach will be cheaper than asking a business attorney create it from scratch—and, realistically, they would probably start with a generic template anyway. Don't rely on your enthusiasm for the idea and your partner; be prudent and smart. Protect yourself and your future by having a proper agreement in place, *signed* by all parties involved.

Once your business is up and running and you start hiring employees, you may want to consider getting an *employment attorney*. Or a bigger payroll provider that offers concierge service can be an option. These firms usually have lawyer-developed agreements, policies, employee manuals, and sexual harassment trainings—whatever is required by your state as well as the federal government. Typically, a good service like that provides everything you need to protect you and your business, while establishing protection for your employees as well.

There are also PEOs (professional employer organizations), which handle all employee-related matters. They essentially lease your employees to you and you pay them a monthly fee for that. They handle payroll processing, employer tax payments, deductions, vacation and sick time, employee manuals and policies, benefits administration, and much more. A company like that may make sense for you down the road because they offer various fringe benefits like health insurance, retirement, life and disability insurance, and transit checks at better prices. These companies have a group of employers like you, so they are able to negotiate a better deal than you could on your own with insurance companies and other providers.

Coaches

As recently as a few years ago I was skeptical when it came to coaches in general. Before I hired my coach I thought I knew it all. (Insert eyeroll here.) I was ignorant, to say the least. I was barely making ends meet despite working a lot and making decent money. During tax season I worked crazy hours and sacrificed family time for clients, some of whom argued with me over $50 in fees. It was terrible. At the time, I had about one hundred clients but still did a lot of free work. I was stressed and it was my own fault. I gave away my knowledge, time, and expertise for less than the agents of a national tax preparation company.

My coach, Chuck Bauer, designed a program with another coach, Jackie Meyer, specifically for accountants. Still, I was skeptical. What could they possible teach *me*? Thankfully, one day they had a free fifty-minute webinar. At the event they shared some of their best tactics, which weren't specifically accounting related but were commonsense things like sending thank-you notes and handwritten cards to prospective clients, as well as a "congrats on your decision to work with us" video to new clients. That call changed my life. I invested in their program. I couldn't afford it at the time but made a return on it of 135 percent within three months. Keep in mind: coaches cannot do the work *for* you. To get results, you must implement what you're taught—otherwise, don't waste your time and money.

The most important thing that coaches did for me was give me a mindset shift. They led me to see that there are other ways of doing business. I learned how to create my packaged services, how to outline scope of work and start charging for services that I previously gave away for free. They also led me to understand that my vision at the time of just having a small practice, all by myself, doing all the work, limited what I could do as a person and as a professional. I sold time for money, gave some away for free, overloaded myself, and did everything on my own. I thought there was no other way, but I realized: *there is always a different and better way to do business.*

If you are just starting off with an idea, you don't need a coach right away, so don't worry. You may not even need one at all, and that's okay. This option will be there for you if you ever need it, so that you never find yourself stuck like I did. In the beginning you will do a lot of the legwork yourself and outline your vision for the future. This will enable you to develop your strategy for how to get there.

The reason many of us need a coach is because we often start a business "just to try things out," as a side gig. We either don't know every aspect of it (sales and marketing was hard for me, so I ignored it) or we keep doing it "the old way" without taking the time to work *on* instead of *in* our business. For example, I was stuck on this notion of having a me-only practice for nearly a decade until I saw how I limited my own potential. Can you relate?

On a piece of paper, write down the goals and beliefs you have today and keep it in a place where you can find it when you feel stuck. When that happens, review your assumptions and wishes. Reexamine whether you really want what you thought you wanted. And if you aren't sure, it may be time to find a coach who will help you ramp up your business, examine your systems, and analyze your assumptions.

You may also experience a mindset shift like I did and find that what you really want has changed and now requires a new approach.

If you decide to explore coaching, know that there are various types of coaches that specialize in specific industries, such as construction, accounting firms, marketing and social media, tech start-ups, real estate, and product sales. Do your due diligence. Yes, all those testimonials and success stories are great, but if a coach—or any professional, for that matter—is confident in their programs, they will do a free session once in a while to share their top tactics and teachings. They won't give out everything they teach, of course, but that's okay; the coaching relationship is personal, so in that complimentary session you will find out two things: whether you like the coach's personality, and whether the few items they shared can be immediately implemented and deliver results for *your* goals. Overall, coaches can be great to take us out of our comfort zone and focus us on what's important.

Accountant-Advisors

We all have this notion of an accountant, this picture in our head when someone says, "I am a CPA." Do you picture someone in a suit, with a briefcase, or in an office with two monitors, a *big* calculator, and a pencil, doing boring work, who is always crazy-busy and works a lot? I know I do, and I am an accountant! Weird, right? But the landscape of what accountants do and what people need has shifted dramatically over the last five to ten years. It happened because the business landscape has changed and now business owners want more advice and support than ever before. A great accountant will play a vital role in your business. They don't just run numbers, keep your books, and file your taxes; it's so much more.

Just as with any professional, accountants may specialize in certain industries, such as e-commerce, construction, daycare centers, restaurants, and professional services. Many bank-based advisors recommend that newborn entrepreneurs find a specialty accountant. As a CPA I never understood why people would want an advisor who specializes in a certain industry. In my experience, professionals who make the biggest mistakes are often very experienced and overly confident. I worked for a door company many years ago that had a fantastic machine operator, a real pro, named Alvaro. His work was precise and top-notch, but one day he nearly cut his finger off with the machine (don't worry, the ER was able to sew it back on and it was as good as new). This was the first time I realized that sometimes people who know their jobs inside and out don't pay as close attention to it as rookies do. This applies to professional services just as much as to manual labor. Dentists, for example, are believed to be at their best when they are in the first five to eight or last ten years of their careers. In the beginning they try hard and work very meticulously, while at the end they don't care as much about money and enjoy their work. Michael McQueen, a prominent data analyst, said it best: "The best asset you've got in any team for revolutionary thought is the person on that team with the freshest eyes."[2] So, I believe that you are better off not looking for a specialty accountant, but rather looking for one who has a fundamental approach and a non-conveyor-belt-style practice.

The accounting industry has changed and a new generation of advisors has officially arrived. The new-generation firms have changed their mindset from the traditional "lots of clients, working on Saturdays, constant hamster wheel" mentality and adopted a way of being a true advisor, a problem-solver, and a solutions-finder. Many of those firms, including mine, have developed a much more rewarding work environment simply because we provide high-value, higher-priced service that gives people like you the support you need.

My firm, for example, gives established businesses clarity and confidence in their operations in several ways. Imagine for a moment that you are our client. We start with learning more about your personal life; this step is important because we are all human and business *is*, in fact, personal. We all bring in our personal lives, sometimes our drama, and our individual aspirations into the business; it's inevitable. For my firm, understanding the basis of your business decisions is critical. There are numerous ways to structure tax and business matters, but there is only one way that is right for *you*. Next, we review your entity structure and income streams. We discuss the best tax planning strategy with you, where your entity structure will minimize your taxes legally. As we learn more about your family and your financial obligations, we help you make use of income-shifting strategies to provide even further tax savings.

Then, we look at your business pricing and offer insights into price psychology, help you experiment with price adjustments, and track results. We help you organize your business operations using our management knowledge and experience and we advise you about potential areas of improvement or redesign of your current structures. We are true efficiency fanatics and love seeing reduction in your business overhead and cost of sales, while you deliver a stellar customer experience to your clients. As accountants, we certainly manage the accounting side of your business, but, first, we set up your books in a way that helps you learn, understand, and own your numbers. My firm will organize your chart of accounts to give you a macro view of your business, while reserving an option to review the micro-level details. In appendix 2 you will find our system of organizing your accounts (which is also downloadable at dreamboldbook.com), so you can set it up right from the start.

Finally, we provide a concierge accounting service to your firm. As an ongoing engagement we update your books either daily or weekly; reconcile monthly; create, with your help, cash flow forecasts; prepare reports; analyze your numbers and then discuss them with you regularly. We strive to give you what you need to see the dynamics of your business's growth. One example of such help is analyzing your marketing spend so that you can better manage and understand it. We help you set realistic goals and track your progress regularly. We periodically review your tax numbers and make sure that the plan we created is still a valid one and adjust it if necessary. And, lastly, we handle all the compliance (in other words, tax filing) work for you.

Certainly, a comprehensive approach like the one I describe is not cheap. To provide this level of service, accountants must get specialized training in tax planning, price psychology, management, top-notch bookkeeping, and tax compliance. Also, professionals of this caliber must invest in themselves, as well: constantly educate themselves, test new technologies, and learn about new industry developments to bring you the best of the best, and all of that costs money and time.

You don't need to invest in this level of service in the very beginning. Until your first month of real operations, even if it's just you or a small team working out of your home office, you won't need many things, but I do encourage you to set up a few spreadsheets to track income, direct material costs, direct labor costs, as well as overhead and the like. You can use the same spreadsheet you used for the ninety-day cash planning in chapter 9.

This book gives you enough resources to ensure you know how to do it yourself but also what to look for in an advisor. In appendix 3 you will find sections describing milestones to watch out for to know when you should hire a top-level advisor. You will also have a list of questions to ask a potential advisor and answers to look for.

If you are at a point where you find yourself needing an advisor now, and if you'd like to find the right advisor for you, go to dreamboldbook.com and check out our directory of professionals. It's free. Firms that our team certifies get the trainings we recommend, so that they can provide great service to you. Advisory firms can't simply pay to be in the directory: their teams have to follow the guidelines, processes, and systems we have established and trained them in. My firm and I will work tirelessly to bring more education, technological developments, and tools to the member-firms, so that you can count on always getting the best strategies available.

12

How Do You Know You're Doing It Right?

MY FEAR OF dentists is real. Ever since I was a kid, my parents felt that painkillers were bad for me, so my teeth were always fixed "naturally," without anesthesia and with awful pain. When I came to the United States, I discovered a flossing tool, so the health of my teeth improved significantly after that. My husband had a different experience: his teeth were always very healthy. When he came to the United States, a "great" doctor was recommended to him. That doctor "fixed" my husband's teeth by opening up and putting fillings into ten previously healthy teeth, all for insurance money.

Taking care of your back office and owning your numbers reminds me of taking care of your teeth. From a young age, many of us are intimidated when it comes to our teeth, yet we are told we must keep them healthy and clean and take care of them regularly so that we have a good, healthy life. Similarly, many of us develop anxiety related to numbers and taxes. Yet, again, you're told that you've got to do it, no matter how unpleasant—and sometimes painful—it is.

You could rely on a recommended professional, but it doesn't always work to your best benefit, especially if you have no way of qualifying that person or a firm. Also, you will need to pay them. Here, my friend, is a little bit of tough love: no matter how painful that initial "fixing" is, or how involved this learning curve will be for the first few steps in your journey, the most successful business owners are those who have nailed their numbers approach. You can do it! Don't look at what others are doing: they are not *you*. So, buckle up and say yes to yourself and your financial health. Just like with teeth, once you get going, it's not such a big deal.

You may, at times, feel like you are a creative mind and you just don't get any of it. You may have not been great at math in school and may feel discouraged along the way, especially in the beginning. To make matters worse, people around you may unload unsolicited advice and recommendations. People closest to you may even mock you or make fun of your desire to understand these basics, and you may find yourself defending your entity choice to a lawyer-friend or saying no to a bookkeeper-friend who offers help for free. But just as you are the only person who can keep your teeth healthy, a brilliant advisor cannot be as passionate about your business as you are.

There will always be people who dismiss how the business landscape has become agile and has changed so much, so that the only way to "make it" is to be revolutionary and forward looking while keeping your finances in order. Pay attention to the most important person in your life: you. Face and embrace that initial tiny pain of deciding to own your numbers and later reap the rewards of being clear and confident in your business, for life and for *any* business you ever start. Doing just a tiny bit every single day, just like brushing and flossing your teeth between visits to the dentist, will reduce the stress of meeting with your accountant and being unpleasantly surprised at tax time. This will protect you from making a money mistake you cannot afford.

The goal of learning your numbers is not to make an accountant out of you. Where you want to be is at a point of running your business with purpose. Before that, you may go through the stages of business-owner growth as it relates to numbers:

- **Stage 1. Basic business.** The learning zone—you're just starting out.

- **Stage 2. Growing business.** The growth zone. You know you're at stage 2 when you realize how much you can grow but you're not getting there because you don't know your money, numbers, and taxes.

- **Stage 3. Focused business.** The down-and-dirty zone. This is probably the most critical stage, so expect to spend most of your time here. At this stage you will do a lot of planning work and develop systems to run your business.

- **Stage 4. Business with intention.** This is the "find your groove" zone. At this stage you will gain your business confidence and develop your own money management routine.

- **Stage 5: Business with purpose.** At last, you are in the powerhouse zone. At this stage, when I ask you how you feel about your bookkeeping, numbers, and taxes, you will say, "I feel confident in my books and in my ability to figure it all out. I know my numbers and have no anxiety about or fear of them. I understand the importance of filing and paying taxes, but I want to pay the lowest amount I owe by law. I have tax and profit reserves to make sure I can always pay my taxes and myself. I have developed and regularly use metrics and reports to track numbers I need to see to manage my business effectively. I review my tax return before I sign it, and I understand what it means. I could teach a child to run this business."

This is a place many small businesses never reach. Can you get there? Yes, you can. Your abilities are limitless and now you know where you are going. If you feel like sharing your commitment to yourself, your dreams, and your vision, send me a quick email at tatiana@tatianatsoir.com with subject line "I faced my numbers," so that I can support you. I am obsessed with when the dots connect in your head, when you see the result of your time, money, and brain investment pay out in a clear vision and confidence in your business. And you can absolutely do this with this book alone. After all, it's just numbers. Should you want a little extra help, you can check out the "Something That's Yours" mini-coaching program that, along with video content, will enable you to ask me questions on our calls and get clarity. You don't have to get it, but it's there if you need it (programs.tatianatsoir.com).

As I talked about this book in advance of its publication, people across the nation, people like you, reached out to me and said, "I wish your book was around when I was starting my business." I kept receiving social media messages asking me when the book was coming out. I believe that every person deserves to follow their passion and build their dream, and the stronger you are, the stronger we all are, and the bigger impact we all can have in the world. The truth is that I wish I could help each and every aspiring business owner, freelancer, or side hustler myself, but it's just not possible. This book, on the other hand, has given you a solid foundation, and I've made it my life's mission to empower you to skip the anxiety and make money doing what you love. The world needs your idea and your voice, so take one step at a time and let's do this.

Appendix 1

Important Terms
You Should Know

Income

When money *comes in*, it's *income*. That's it. Whenever you get money for something you do or sell, it's income. If you inherit money, that's income, too, but you don't pay tax on it. Similarly, if you sue someone and get a settlement, it's income and sometimes you don't pay tax on that, either. There are several different kinds of income. It can be gross income, gross profit ("Wait, I thought income and profit are the same things? Huh?"), top-line income, taxable income, net operating income, net income, bottom-line income, other income, nontaxable income, and different type of income. Then there is also EBITDA... Wait, what? You'll see.

Gross income

When we talk about *gross income*, it is the same as *revenue* and *top-line income*. In English it means that it is the total sales of your goods or services and it does *not* include any expenses or direct costs you have to pay to *be able to sell*. This is just an indicator of your *volume*. Unfortunately, many businesses and business owners focus on this top line/gross income/revenue. It breaks my heart to watch them remain in that mindset and run their business into the ground. If you remember Angela's story, that's exactly what happened: she focused on the top line and didn't have the discipline to make sure that the bottom line was also taken care of. Net income is a much better indicator of a business's health, so don't repeat her mistake—don't focus on growing your top line at all costs. Sure, the top line is an important number, but would you rather have $2 million in gross income with $100,000 in profits or $500,000 in gross income with $100,000 in profits? It seems that the former is a whole lot more effort for the same bottom line, so I would take the latter any day of the week, wouldn't you?

Gross profit

Gross profit is an important number if you have any kind of direct costs. It's your top-line revenue minus your direct costs. *Direct costs*, sometimes referred to as *variable costs*, are costs that you *only* have to pay if you are making sellable products or services and making *any sales*. If you produce clothes, for example, your direct costs might include material (fabric), a design team (production staff), shipping to your warehouse, warehouse storage fees, and much more, but you get the idea. If you are a professional services company, let's say an interior design firm, your direct costs might include design staff, cost of furniture sales (if you sell it as part of the design, and many designers do), and quality control costs. You get the picture, I hope.

Gross profit gives you an important indicator of your efficiency: *the gross profit percentage*. That tells you the percent of the "leftover" income you have to (1) pay your fixed expenses (rent, utilities, admin staff, professional fees, travel, and so on); (2) pay yourself; and (3) have a good leftover *net income* to either invest back into your business or take for yourself.

Taxable income

Leave this one for your tax professional, but, in a nutshell, this is a number on which your further tax due is calculated. It is hard for you to know that number by simply looking at your internal reports, but it is largely influenced by tax law and how certain expenses count as "ordinary and necessary." If your bookkeeper or accountant knows their stuff, your chart of accounts, also known as your list of categories, will be set up so that you can see your estimated taxable income for a current or a past period you are reviewing.

Nontaxable income

This should also be left for your accountant to deal with. There are different kinds, such as municipal bond interest in your home state, but it's not something you can learn quickly and, frankly, it could change anyway. Just know that either this income is not taxed or there are some special (aka magic) rules that apply.

Other income

This is generally considered income *other than* your normal business income, which depends on what you do. For a business that sells toys, other income would include interest, in other words, those measly few bucks a bank pays you in interest when you hold money in it long enough. On the other hand, if you are a bank, interest income is your regular income, while selling a toy would be "other."

The difference between net income and net operating income

Your *bottom line* and *net operating income* are, for our purposes, the exact same thing, said differently. Simple, right? *Net income* is the bottom-bottom line, after *everything*, including other income (see above). *Net operating income* is *before* other income and other expenses, so net operating income tells you how much your business generated by simply *operating, or being in business.* I like this number because it ignores supplemental "stuff" (like interest, other expenses, depreciation) and shows us the "real deal." If you are losing money in operations, then supplementing that by earning a little something on the side will not last you long.

EBITDA

Don't worry about this one right now. It only means *earnings before interest, taxes, depreciation, and amortization,* and unless you're a publicly traded company, just don't worry about it. Chances are, if you are going to go public, there will be other people to worry about this number, not you. So, forget you ever saw it.

Expenses

Cost of sales

These are known as *cost of goods sold*, and are also known as *direct costs*, as we discussed above; we use them to get the gross profit. Those direct costs are similar to those variable costs we saw before.

Normal expenses

These are the ordinary and necessary and can range from advertising to rent to telephone. When you subtract these from your income, you get net operating income.

Other expenses

These are things out of the normal course of business. An example would be a rental real estate company with a sale of one of the properties managed: the normal course of business is rental and all expenses related to that (mortgage interest, taxes, maintenance, repairs, and so on), while a sale of one unit in a block of units rented, all under the same entity, presumably, would be listed as other income and other (related) expenses for your reporting purposes. In this case, it's a different type of income for tax purposes as well, so it pays to show it separately, after the main operations' numbers.

Other Important Terms

There are a couple of words and things that you just need to be aware of.

Assets

Sometimes when you buy or spend money on something, it's not an immediate expense and deduction for taxes. If your purchase is used for more than just one accounting period (generally, a year), you have to allocate the cost over that period of time and are not allowed to deduct it in full right away.

So, if you are starting a restaurant and just bought all the mixers, racks, and pots, they may not be an immediate expense for tax purposes, and they definitely go on to a balance sheet (as opposed to a profit and loss statement, discussed later) as an asset. An asset is something that is used in business but is not immediately consumed. Napkins for a restaurant would be an expense (not an asset), whereas kitchenware like bowls and pots can be used for years and are assets and therefore need to be depreciated.

Assets are also other things like your start-up expenses, for example, organizational fees, your equipment, furniture, computers, cars and trucks, large tools, buildings, as well as some basic things like bank accounts and receivables—in other words, what customers owe you on terms like net 30 days.

Liabilities

Liabilities are things that also don't show up on your income statement, also known as a profit and loss; they're basically your debts—what you owe people, banks, vendors, and lenders.

Equity

Equity is what's left that's yours. You were probably confused before and I most likely lost you just now. To explain this concept, I like to use the basic accounting equation:

$$Assets - Liabilities = Equity$$

In case of a home you purchase, this looks like this:

$$Home - Mortgage = What you own$$

So, when you purchase a home using a mortgage, until you've paid off the mortgage you don't own the home outright. You own it jointly with a bank and each of you is entitled to your share of this asset. Your equity is the share of it you currently own.

Appendix 2

A Do-It-Yourself Tool for Seeing the Big Picture

DO I REALLY Need to Do Accounting?

A popular opinion going around is that accounting is useless, that looking at the past is not helpful or useful, but I disagree with that. We set up our books in a certain way to be able to set goals, monitor our progress toward them, and understand where mistakes or abnormalities happen so that we can course-correct as needed. The ability to make fast decisions when something isn't going the way you planned is priceless, and to have that ability you must create a foundation in the form of a good record-keeping system. It may seem too simple or meaningless in the beginning, but what you are doing is building up history, which you will later use to track your progress, build forecasts of cash flows, and analyze trends.

What Software Should I Use?

I have a long-standing preference when it comes to software. Unlike many accountants, I started my career path as a bookkeeper and got my first bookkeeping experience at a small plumbing company. There I handled every aspect of the business: payroll, bookkeeping, paperwork, contracts, and payments, all while going to school to study accounting. Many basics that professors taught I applied immediately to my work. For several years, I had a small bookkeeping business and I had to work with a variety of software packages, yet I fell in love with Intuit's QuickBooks product.

Here is an important disclaimer: No software is perfect, and there are always little kinks that your bookkeeper or accountant must be aware of to help you manage your business better. Over the years QuickBooks has grown to be a pretty powerful accounting tool for small businesses and has definitely become my favorite. I don't work for Intuit, nor do I get any compensation for mentioning its product. My opinion is based solely on a decade and a half of experience in the bookkeeping and accounting trenches. I recommend QuickBooks Online (QBO) software to every business owner, because it's a robust and easy-to-use platform for your business finances.

You don't need QBO when you are developing and building out your idea blueprint; save the money and wait. Use a spreadsheet for the first few months or maybe even years and track your income and expenses there. As soon as you hit a mark of fifty transactions per month, purchase a QBO software subscription or a similar-level product.

How Do I Set Up My Accounts?

In a new bookkeeping system you usually get a standard chart of accounts, where accounts in the same category are listed alphabetically. However, every business is different, so it would be impossible for a software developer to predict and build a custom list for every possible business; it's up to the accounting advisors and bookkeepers, as well as the business owners, to set up a system that works well for them. That's exactly what I will help you do here. A method I use has been proven very powerful: organize expense accounts in blocks of related ones, so that you can look at the big picture while examining the fussy details when you need to.

Since in many software packages accounts are often organized alphabetically, I thought it would make sense to use numbers to organize them in groups. Use this example and tweak it for your business (see page 175); if you'd like the resource, you can download it free from dreamboldbook.com.

For these purposes, items 2 through 8 should be set up as expense account types and with the number and name in CAPS. These will represent blocks of expenses, so that you can get a big-picture understanding easily, when you need it. Let's review what each of these categories can include and the best way to look at them. When you set this up, the items with numbers will be accounts, while detailed expenses will be subaccounts of these groups. Remember, this is all flexible, and you can adapt it to fit your business. You may not have direct expenses—line 1—at all, if you provide the service yourself.

1   **Direct expenses** is to address **variable costs**. If, all of a sudden, you stop producing and selling your product or a service, your variable costs would be zero.

2   **Marketing, promotional, and business development** will include things like advertising, which can have subcategories of its own—for example, digital advertising, print mailers, TV. It also includes promotional items and related costs (flyers, brochures, and posters), client gifts (there are limitations on the dollar value of gifts per client for those gifts to be tax deductible) and business development trips and meetings.

3   For **staff expenses** you will set up several accounts, such as wages, payroll taxes, health insurance, and other benefits. You will most likely not have all of these in the beginning, but it's quite possible that your business will need labor right away.

4   **Travel expenses** should include, separately, travel such as air, hotel, and car rental, which may be set up as sub-subaccounts; local travel (taxis and car service around town); and meals. For better tracking, meals can be separated into a few different kinds, such as travel meals, office meals, and business meals, but do create a meals account and set up those under this main one. This will make your accountant's job at year-end easier and will give you a better understanding of how much you spend on different kinds of meals. Under travel you will also set up car and auto expenses and create subaccounts for gas, car insurance, tolls, and parking.

5   **Owner compensation** is not an intuitive one but is important. If you remember the entities from chapter 7, I have a slight preference for S corporations. Regardless of the entity type, you will take the money for yourself—after all, you *are* in business to make money, right? If you choose to be an S corporation, you will need to pay yourself through payroll a certain reasonable amount. Now, at the very start, in your first year, you may not make enough to warrant a payroll service

and that's okay. Do set up the accounts, though, because if you're running your business right you will soon be taking money for yourself—and, I bet, a significant amount.

6 **General and administrative** is a catchall category. Here you would set up and track expenses like rent, bank charges, dues and subscriptions, postage, printing fees (unless it's marketing), telephone, utilities, and insurance. This is your overhead.

7 **Professional fees** can go into **staff expenses**, but I prefer tracking them separately. Here you will create subcategories for legal, accounting, bookkeeping, administrative, coaching, and IT fees paid to outside providers. If any of these professionals become your full-time employees, you will change their posting to be under staff expenses at that time.

8 **Business taxes, interest, and licenses** will be for interest you pay on credit cards or loans, state entity-level income taxes, various licensing fees, and the like. I would set these up as detailed as possible.

9 **Other income** is for items like interest the bank pays you and other miscellaneous receipts that are not part of your ongoing business.

10 **Donations** should all be set up as **other expenses** in your accounting system, as should HSA (Health Savings Account) contributions and pensions. This should not be a part of your operating income. Donations are self-explanatory; make sure that you have a receipt in the form of a letter from the organization. Watch out for sponsorships: I've had clients tell me that those are charitable, but the reality is that, although when you sponsor a charitable event you *are* doing a good deed, it's a marketing expense, not a donation. Donations are heavily scrutinized during audits, so don't make a mistake.

It has to be a pure donation with nothing in return. A charity dinner is partially deductible, but the organization will tell you in the letter how much of the ticket price is deductible.

IF YOU SET UP your chart this way you will be able to see a macro view of your business, which is important for big-picture planning and strategy. At the same time, you can plan your month, quarter, and year and look for ways to save money and identify groups where closer attention must be paid at different times throughout the course of your business.

	Month 1
Sales of products/services	$20,000
A. Total Revenue	**$20,000**
1. Direct expenses/labor/materials	$5,000
Gross Margin (Total Revenue – Direct Expenses)	**$15,000**
2. Marketing, promo, and biz dev	$100
3. Staff expenses	$0
4. Travel expenses	$200
5. Owner compensation	$1,000
6. General and admin (G&A)	$750
7. Professional fees	$1,500
8. Business taxes, interest, licenses	$250
B. Total Expenses (2 Through 8)	**$3,800**
9. Other income (+)	$5
10. Donations, etc. (-)	$50
C. Other Income (Net)	**($45)**
Net Income (A – 1 – B + C)	**$11,155**

Appendix 3

Milestones

The Early Days

As you are just starting out, you don't need to spend a lot of money on keeping your books, which is great news. When you have a designated business account and credit cards, following business expenses becomes easier, so start with that. In fact, separating business and personal transactions into separate accounts is probably the best thing you can do early on.

Even if you operate as a freelancer or under your own name, get a second bank account and designate one credit card to be business only. It becomes critical during tax time and in case of an audit. Here is what I mean: when personal income and expenses are mixed in with business, it's impossible to prove that certain deposits, where someone reimbursed you for their share of dinner or rent, were nonbusiness. Similarly, if you purchased supplies and didn't keep a receipt, it will be hard to assert to an auditor that *these* ones were for business and *those* were for your home. During tax time it is much easier to go through only transactions within your business account and classify them, as opposed to going through all your transactions for the year and trying to remember which ones were business.

Use the resources available with this book to break down monthly transactions into those categories and you'll be in good shape. Download them at dreamboldbook.com.

Do I Need an Accountant?

For your first year on your own you don't need a full-blown accounting firm, but I would recommend getting a professional involved. A solo certified public accountant (CPA) or an enrolled agent (EA) will have the foundational tax filing knowledge and should be able to file your taxes without issues. Do check your tax documents, because when a practitioner files hundreds of tax returns in a three-month period, mistakes are inevitable. As you grow, you can later hire a professional who is a new-generation advisor. They will be your support team and can help you with pricing, management, hiring, accounting, and systems, all while keeping taxes in mind.

It may be a year or two before you hire someone of that caliber. In the meantime, you'll need to find a professional who will do the due diligence and file your annual income taxes, and, possibly, sales and payroll taxes as well. You must file all the paperwork required regularly, so don't lead yourself to believe that just because you didn't "make" money, you don't have to file. It's all about the disclosure, and the money you invested in your business can provide a tax benefit to you at the end of the year.

What if I Hire People?

If you have to hire employees, I recommend getting a full-service payroll provider. Don't get a service where you process payroll and then have to remember to file government forms and pay taxes separately. You will make mistakes, you will underpay, and you will struggle to make a monthly payment because it will be a big chunk at once. Find a service to do it all for you.

Your other option is to use one of the big companies, but I prefer smaller payroll providers: their customer service is often much better. Keep in mind: If you experience sharp growth in your business (yay!) and have to scale quickly, don't switch payroll providers mid-year. Save yourself the headache and do so at the end of your business year. If you absolutely have to switch during the year, do so at a quarter-end. The same idea applies if you switch entities or entity types as part of your organization: do that at year-end.

What Else Do I Need to Worry About?

A few words about nexus. Nexus is literally a connection linking several things together, and when it comes to taxation, nexus is your business's connection to a certain state. States have to make money to fund all their operations and programs, so they are particular about businesses operating within their borders. Seek professional help if you cross states' borders during your business operations. This includes your employees and exclusive contractors working out of another state, employees delivering products or services to another state, having an independent warehouse, and keeping inventory in a state or being a "remote seller" of goods into another state.

Typically, your accountant will need to perform a periodic review of nexus and register you within states with which a connection has been established. As you grow and sell more, you will need to pay attention to sales to each and every state, so create systems ahead of time that will ensure you are tracking your sales, employees, and locations properly.

Bookkeeping Milestones

Up to fifty transactions per month

Bookkeeping is important, and it's not as hard as you think—remember, it's just numbers. As you grow, you have a choice: you *may* manage bookkeeping yourself, but if you are at a point of *more than fifty to sixty transactions per month*, you should get a real bookkeeper. It can be a remote or in-person service or a combination of both. In the beginning you should keep a tight grip on paying bills yourself. Over the years I've found that it is a very effective technique for business owners to keep an eye on cash and be strategic about managing it by paying bills personally. You definitely want to keep signing checks.

Up to one hundred transactions per month

When you're close to the threshold of *one hundred transactions per month*, you definitely need a bookkeeper. If you don't get one, you will spend more of your time working *in* your business instead of working *on* it. You may find it challenging to assess and determine the quality of a bookkeeper or to do any sort of verification of their skills and knowledge.

To become a bookkeeper, a person doesn't need any specific training. Knowing a software system often becomes a substitute for formal bookkeeping training. Software solutions with nice-looking interfaces are often part of the problem. When a bookkeeper has learned how to use the software, yet does not understand what is happening on the back end of the interface, it's a recipe for failure. I've seen it happen to numerous clients before they came to my firm.

The results of badly done bookkeeping aren't always easily discovered. They often emerge as missed tax deductions and over- or under-reported income, and besides possibly resulting in a higher tax and a higher audit risk, they provide no useful information for you to better manage your business and make decisions.

How to find the right bookkeeper

Because I started out as a bookkeeper, I have intimate knowledge of all the intricacies that come up in bookkeeping, and, being an advisor, I use bookkeeping as one of my top tools for tax savings and business management. As Will Durant writes, paraphrasing the Greek philosopher Aristotle, excellence "is not an act but a habit."[1] Get a professional with a proven track record of excellence, someone committed to making excellence a habit. You can easily spot people like that.

Over the years, I have worked with numerous bookkeepers. Those who were good often built businesses and delegated their work, so either the work quality decreased or the client had to go to a different person at a bookkeeper's firm for a different tax, and that's painful.

If you want to find a bookkeeper on your own or you already have a candidate, here is how you tell whether or not they are right for you. The most important part is their problem-solver mindset, so look for that. Also, keep that account-subaccount setup in mind when you talk to them. Ask your candidate the following questions and listen to how they respond:

- **How would you set up the chart of accounts so that I can look at my business at both the micro and the macro level?**

Yes, they may "cheat" and get the setup structure from this book, but in doing so they will strive to transform into a problem-solver as opposed to just a journal entry processor, so it's a good thing.

- **What's the difference between an asset, a liability, and an equity? Provide an example.**

An asset can be cash in the bank or inventory. Liabilities are debts and credit cards. And equity is best illustrated in terms of a home purchase. A home you buy is an asset, your asset, something that is *yours*. A mortgage is a portion of your home's purchase price that you owe your bank (a liability) and the difference between the two (home value less mortgage amount) is your equity, what you own in your house. It's a simplified explanation but it makes sense. Look for something similar in the answer.

- **Why do we have fixed assets, current assets, other assets, and a separate type of account, accounts receivable?**

This question is more software-related; nevertheless, you might as well ask. Fixed assets are things like furniture, computers, fixtures in the place of business, cars and trucks (unless they are leased). Fixed assets depreciate over several years, depending on the kind, so there is a depreciation expense associated with them. Current assets include short-term loans you give, prepaid items (if you prepay an expense, it's not immediately deductible in certain cases), and inventory.

Other assets include those that don't fit into the other ones: they are not cash in the bank, not fixed assets. Examples include the rent security deposit you paid and intangible items like trademarks or patents. Accounts receivable is a whole other animal. Technically, it is part of the current assets: it includes invoices you've issued that haven't yet been paid.

- **Why do we have separate account types, and what's the difference between accounts payable, current liabilities, and long-term liabilities?**

Accounts payable is for bills you receive; they become a payable, in other words, due to be paid. It's what you owe in the normal course of business. For a product-based business it will be factory bills, and for a service-based business it will be outside service consultant bills. Current liabilities are debts that are due in one year or less, like short-term loans you receive or credit card balances. Long-term liabilities are loans and debts due in more than one year.

- **What's an equity account? What does it represent?**

Remember my analogy of a home purchase? Equity is the difference between what your home is worth and what you owe the bank. In a business, it's what's left after all debts are paid.

- **What is a balance sheet? What's the significance of it? How is it helpful to a business owner?**

A balance sheet is a report of your financial position at a point in time. This report doesn't show you information for a certain period; it tells you, if you were to close your doors today, how much in assets you would have to pay off all your debts and keep what's left. The balance sheet is most helpful to look at on a month-to-month basis and analyze how it changes.

- **What is reconciliation and why does it need to be done?**

Reconciliation is often confused with expense categorization. The process of reconciliation is comparing your book bank register with your bank statement to identify any missing or duplicated items of money coming in and going out. After you have done the reconciliation and your difference is zero, look at the uncleared items to determine why they aren't cleared. Sometimes the checks were written late in the month and vendors haven't yet deposited them. If those uncleared items are deposits or really old checks, a proper reversal needs to be done without affecting the last filed tax return.

- **When performing a reconciliation, what would you do if you had a difference?**

If you had a difference, you would start by checking the basics: your beginning balance, your ending balance, and statement ending date—do all three match the bank statement? If those are correct, you would uncheck all the items and redo the reconciliation, starting with deposits and making sure that the total deposits match the statement. Then you would do the same with outgoing funds.

- **Is it okay to have negative numbers on your balance sheet or profit and loss statements? What would you do if you saw them?**

It's *not okay*. If you run your profit and loss or balance sheet reports and see negative numbers, something was done wrong and needs to be investigated. I would also investigate any meaningless categories of expenses, such as purchases (it's a generic term that tells me nothing about what it is), miscellaneous (again, nothing specific), or my all-time favorite, reimbursements. That category should never exist on its own. For example, when you reimburse a specific expense like travel, meals, or education, book it as that expense. So, when you're writing a check to someone to reimburse them for a taxi they had to take, you assign a local travel expense to it, and not a reimbursement expense.

THERE ARE MORE questions, but these will give you a good start. If the bookkeeper you find is a great one, they will continuously acquire new skills and develop new ways to help their clients thrive, so hold on to them.

It makes sense to continue to have a bookkeeper plus a once-a-year-tax-preparer setup until your reach $200,000 in *net income* per year. After that you will need to replace your regular tax preparer with a new-generation advisor, because over this threshold you may be missing out on tax benefits and savings that require advanced training in tax planning, as well as other things like price psychology and cash management. Don't worry, you will still need your bookkeeper—as I said, bookkeeping is important—so hold on to that great person you've found.

What's next?

If you've crossed this major threshold of $200,000 *net income*, you are on solid ground and I want to say *congratulations*! You are operating and growing your business and now are ready for a more involved support system. A traditional accounting firm typically has conveyor-belt-type operations, and at this stage you've effectively outgrown them.

The most important qualifier for a new-generation advisor is working with fewer clients more extensively and regularly.

The era of "cranking out returns" accounting service is over, so ask your candidates questions and pay attention to their goals. Are they looking to grow exponentially?

A better and more extensive service, as you have probably guessed, will be more expensive but is a much better deal for you if you want a real coach. This kind of professional will be your advisor and sounding board to help you see the consequences of your ideas and will offer a different point of view on the subject.

Ideally, an accountant-advisor is a CPA or an EA (see earlier in this section) who is also trained in advanced tax planning strategies. These strategies have been somewhat discussed throughout the book, but make sure the candidate is familiar with income-shifting, entity-restructuring, and benefits-maximization strategies, so they can serve you well.

Several organizations train accountants in advanced tax planning, among them the American Institute of Certified Tax Planners and Tax Master Network. These organizations issue certifications based on trainings and provide ongoing education on new tax developments. Furthermore, you will want your advisor to be familiar with the intricacies of managing and forecasting cash. That's a super-important aspect of any business, so you'll want someone with knowledge and a systematic approach.

A real advisor

Your advisor should help you set up your cash flow forecast and review progress with you regularly. They should be working with you at least monthly or even weekly. Together you will work closely to identify areas where you should cut expenses, so that you know which subscriptions or services you need to reevaluate and possibly cancel; which vendors to contact and work out a payment plan for the past-due bills;

and determine if your price points are right and test price increases on a limited basis and then analyze results.

In a perfect world, a true advisor will have some business management training, such as a master's in business administration degree or a certificate. However, training via experience working in the trenches of a business will work just as well; just remember Michael McQueen's words and his "freshest eyes" approach[2]—often a highly specialized professional isn't always best.

You should take your time when selecting an advisor. Don't rush, but also trust your gut. I've had prospective client calls where I was eager to take on the client, but my gut said they wouldn't be a good personality fit, and I was right. I learned all that after making a few mistakes, taking on clients who didn't listen to or value my advice and who blamed others for their choices. Your advisor should become your partner and care about your business almost as much as you do. Such a professional will not be able to service many clients, and that's a great thing. They will also focus on building life-long relationships with their clients' other advisors, such as financial advisors, pension administrators, and attorneys.

How to find the right advisor

When you are interviewing a potential advisor, pay close attention to whether they talk about things you need to get done (like bookkeeping and tax filing, in other words, compliance) as opposed to the things you want, such as legal strategies for tax reduction that save you money, cash stability and profit growth, and bottom-line goal orientation. Ask them whether they think a $1 million gross a year is a good business and whether you should strive for $4 million and see what they say. If they say, "Whatever you would like," or "If you think this is what you want," or something of that nature, they are not a new-generation advisor. If they say, "Well, your gross is impressive, but are you profitable? How profitable are you?" you may have found a good advisor. Nobody will know everything, but great advisors know what they don't know, so they will help you hire a specialist when they feel one is needed.

If you want to skip the hard work, I have made it a little easier for you and created a system of certifying firms to become the new-generation advisors. The great thing is that firms cannot pay to be listed in this directory: they have to go through a vetting process and get certified in several independent programs, so that I can be sure they will bring their best to you. You can find an accountant or a bookkeeper for you at dreamboldbook.com.

There is a reason I decided to create a directory for you. For a while I couldn't understand why preparers who do substandard work often believe they are great and are overly self-confident. It's hard for anyone to evaluate another professional's skills adequately, especially you as a client, who isn't yet well-versed in taxes. You hope they're as good as they say, or you rely on a recommendation from a friend.

Why is there a range of professionals?

Recently I stumbled upon what's called the Dunning-Kruger effect, which illustrates how people in any industry develop their knowledge. Check it out on the next page.

It seems that at the very beginning of our professional accountant journey (I am sure it applies to other professions, too), our confidence goes up pretty high. After all, we know so much, right? Wrong. We often don't know what we don't know, and that's a real problem. As we get more experience, our confidence decreases, and we realize that there is "more to it." At some point we reach a state of desperation and think that we know absolutely nothing. And only after we become

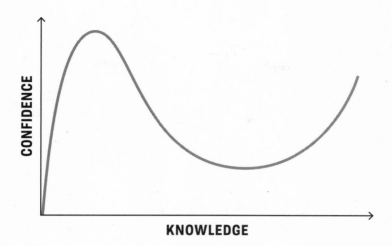

true experts and have been "around the block" a few times does our confidence come back up slowly. I've certainly gone through this curve and all its stages and had a mentor on my speed dial to help me learn what I didn't know.

When you speak with an advisor or a tax preparer, keep an ear out for over-confidence not substantiated by things you can understand. Figure out if the confidence comes from that initial peak, or is it the second, lower peak that comes with experience and learning. Ask clarifying questions and don't be afraid to look silly: if you don't ask questions now, you may end up regretting it later.

True experts almost never have one definite answer for a seemingly easy question. It's nearly always an "it's complicated" and long—that is, if you want to get to the bottom of your issue. Yes, I know, it is sometimes a little boring to listen to, but it's in your interest to stop the person and ask them to explain or rephrase until you "get it." If they are true masters, that's when they'll speak in a way that is clear and simple.

Acknowledgments

I THINK THAT IT'S great fortune to have great teachers in your life, and I have been very fortunate to have met some of the best ones that ever existed.

I'm forever grateful to my parents, who pushed me to be better and who shoved me into a school that had eight hours of English per week since day one. It transformed my future back then and it has had an impact on my life and career since. Thank you for loving me for who I am.

Thank you, Svetlana Asinova, the fearless and tough English teacher, an Educator with a capital E. Because of you, I got to the level of English that made it possible for me to write my book. Also, in my first year of college, I was correcting the English teacher's grammar all the time (she probably hated me for it—oh well).

My journey in numbers started when I chose math as my major in middle school. My teacher Marina Falevich is not only a phenomenal math educator, but she also has a passion for making math a part of your life and she influenced my love for it. I am forever thankful, Marina, for your expert guidance and for allowing me to learn calculus while in high school, which enabled me to excel in every math class since and develop a love for numbers. I am forever grateful for your passion for your students' success.

My passion for math continued into college, where I met yet another phenomenal math teacher, Olga Vyarvilskaya, who took my numbers skills to the next level and had a lot of patience for my self-diagnosed ADD. I thank you, dear O.N.

My journey in accounting began and was transformed by an extraordinary teacher, Stephani Mason. Although I was scared of failing your Principles II class when I first met you, Stephani, something you said changed my life and my career: you said "excellence is a matter of choice; so is mediocrity" in one of your accounting classes and I chose to excel since then in everything I have done. I am forever thankful to you for allowing me to see what's possible.

My book journey started because of Mike Michalowicz, and I thank you, Mike, for having that Author Up event and giving me an insider's look into the world of being an author. Because of this event I set out to write a life-changing book. And thank you for introducing me to AJ Harper. She's phenomenal.

I thank you, AJ Harper, for your nurturing guidance throughout this process and your motherly love for me and my book. This book wouldn't have been possible without you. Hugs!

Laura Stone, a passionate supporter of authors who set out to change lives with their books, I thank you! Your energy is contagious and it helped me keep on going.

Thank you, Page Two, my wonderful publisher: Trena, Gabi, Chris, Kendra, Taysia, and Peter, you have guided me through this process and supported my work. It would have been super-hard without you guys.

Thank you, James Harbeck, my editor, for your gentle and nurturing edits. I love that my voice was preserved and amplified by your edits and cannot thank you enough for that.

I thank all my clients, past, present, and future. Your eagerness to learn, your out-of-the-box approaches and leadership styles, and your great journey in entrepreneurship have been a blessing to be a part of. I am honored to have been serving all of you.

I want to thank my team, who have helped me manage everything and not lose my mind. Oxana, Kristina, Daniel, Nadia, and Amber, you guys are awesome!

To my PR consultants, the phenomenal Angela Bonnici, the great Chris Winfield and Jen Gottlieb, and Rachel Wright, who have helped me put my passion into words and be clear on my message. That triggered clarity in other areas of my business and life, so I thank you.

I thank you, fellow authors and 6-a.m.-writing-sprint-buddies. Your stories and support have been life-changing and your kindness I will remember forever. I will also support you and your books in every way I can.

I thank my uncles Volodya and Lenya; aunt Marina (I have two of them, so both); my cousins (late) Sergey, Andrey, and Natasha; Grandpas Sasha and Benedikt; and Grandma Zina for wonderful childhood memories.

My Grandpa Yuzik, who raised me as his own grandchild (funny story, it wasn't really a secret but until I was sixteen years old I didn't know he wasn't my blood-grandpa) and loved me so much, I know you won't be able to read this, but I will come and translate this for you, I promise. I love you.

My best friends, Kristina, Katya, Nadia, Kostik, and Sveta, you guys tolerate my dark and dirty sense of humor and support me in everything I set out to do. Without you it wouldn't have been the same. I mean, my singing wouldn't have been the same! Till next time at a karaoke, ladies!

My mentor and my true fan Rick Schaffer and his wife, Barbara. We met at a Hunter College reception since you sponsored my scholarship in honor of your mom, Geraldine

Schaffer. Despite making me cry during that first meeting, you have helped me and my family tremendously and I will always remember your kindness.

My mentors and coaches Jackie Meyer and Chuck Bauer: you guys allowed me to see what's possible for me and taught me to take my life back. I am forever grateful for your guidance. My family is, too.

My fellow accounting geeks, Sweta Adkin and Diego Rodriguez. I can't wait to argue about an IRC section with you and geek out over tax stuff. You rock!

To the late Zvi Michaeli, a young Jewish boy, whom my family hid during World War II, risking their lives, I thank you for allowing me to be a part of your family here in the United States (Nancy, Doron, and Ashley) and for connecting me with my history and the family I would never have found on my own. It makes me proud to know that in my blood there is a vein of the great people, Mikhalina and Wladyslaw Woewodzki, whose names are forever engraved on the wall at the Garden of the Righteous Among the Nations at Yad Vashem in Israel. I was lucky to find Genya, Galina, Jadvyga, Agnieszka, and Marius, family I haven't known for many years. Your story, Zvi, will never be forgotten, and neither will the story of your wife, Paula, who went through hell at the concentration camp. My family and my kids will know and remember you and Paula forever.

I thank my wonderful talented sister Kate, who has taken phenomenal photos of me (you know, those professional headshots where I look fabulous?) and helped me film many educational videos and make everything I create look top-notch. It would have been hard without you. And Hazel, Aiden, and Yerke certainly helped, too. (By not being around when you and I worked!)

I thank my late grandma, Nadia, who didn't live long enough to meet my children and see my book come out. I do think you would be very proud of who I've become. You loved me obsessively; it should be illegal to love someone other than your child as much as you loved me. And I always loved you back just as much.

Most importantly, my husband, Leo. Thank you for being patient with my passion-driven temperament and supporting my journey in numbers since the very beginning. It's a gift in life to have a father like you and our kids are so lucky, as am I. And our dog and chicks, too. I will love you forever, soul mate.

Notes

Chapter 1: Your Dream Awaits

1   Such as Edward Ugel's *Money for Nothing: One Man's Journey Through the Dark Side of Lottery Millions* (New York: Harper Business, 2008).

2   Sandra Grauschopf, "Lottery Curse Victims: 7 People Who Won Big & Lost Everything," *The Balance Everyday*, April 27, 2020, thebalance everyday.com/lottery-curse-victims-896653.

3   See Associated Press, "NY Lawyer Pleads Guilty to Preparing False Tax Return," *Washington Times*, December 2, 2014, washingtontimes.com/news/2014/dec/2/ny-lawyer-pleads-guilty-to-preparing-false-tax-ret/.

Chapter 3: Do You Know Your Risks?

1   Kat Eschner, "The Bizarre Story of 'Vasa,' the Ship That Keeps On Giving," *Smithsonian Magazine*, August 10, 2017, smithsonianmag.com/smart-news/bizarre-story-vasa-ship-keeps-giving-180964328/.

2   Find out more at, among other places, *Encyclopaedia Britannica*, s.v., "John Wilkinson," last updated July 10, 2020, britannica.com/biography/John-Wilkinson.

Chapter 6: Should You Get Investors?

1   Donald Miller, *Building a StoryBrand: Clarify Your Message so Customers Will Listen* (New York: HarperCollins, 2017).

2   Brian Cohen and John Kador, *What Every Angel Investor Wants You to Know: An Insider Reveals How to Get Smart Funding for Your Billion-Dollar Idea* (New York: McGraw-Hill, 2013), 58.

Chapter 7: Step One: Create Your Legal Entity

1   "26 U.S. Code § 1202—Partial Exclusion for Gain from Certain Small Business Stock," Legal Information Institute, Cornell Law School, accessed September 29, 2020, law.cornell.edu/uscode/text/26/1202.

2   David S. Rose, *The Startup Checklist: 25 Steps to a Scalable, High-Growth Business* (New York: Wiley, 2016), 90-92.

3   "Pass-through entity" simply means that there is no separate federal tax on the entity. This kind of entity only files an informational tax return with the IRS. The income and losses pass through to the owners and are reported and taxed on each owner's personal tax filing.

Chapter 8: Step Two: Determine Your Price Strategy

1   "History," Warby Parker, accessed August 31, 2020, warbyparker.com/history.

2   Margaret Heffernan, "Why Did Tesco Fail in the US?" CBS News, September 12, 2013, cbsnews.com/news/why-did-tesco-fail-in-the-us.

3   Mark Wickersham, *Price: The Fastest Way to Change Profits* (self-published, 2017), 22-24.

4   Leigh Caldwell, *The Psychology of Price: How to Use Price to Increase Demand, Profit and Customer Satisfaction* (New York: Crimson Publishing, 2012), 32.

5   Dan Ariely, *Predictably Irrational: The Hidden Forces That Shape Our Decisions* (New York: HarperCollins, 2010), 2-6.

6   Read about this in "The Importance of Irrelevant Alternatives," *The Economist*, May 22, 2009, economist.com/democracy-in-america/2009/05/22/the-importance-of-irrelevant-alternatives.

7   Caldwell, *The Psychology of Price*, 68.

8   Paul Lee, "The Williams-Sonoma Bread Maker: A Case Study," *Wall Street Journal*, April 10, 2013, blogs.wsj.com/accelerators/2013/04/10/paul-lee-the-williams-sonoma-bread-maker-a-case-study/.

Chapter 9: Step Three: Set Up Your "Cash Is King" Routine

1 Mike Michalowicz, *Profit First: Transform Your Business from a Cash-Eating Monster to a Money-Making Machine* (New York: Portfolio, 2017), 23.

2 In the Programs section of my website, you will find the work sprints I started for people like you to get a little extra help in the process of becoming a business owner and learning your numbers. See programs .tatianatsoir.com for details.

Chapter 11: Step Five: Know When to Seek Help

1 Rose, *The Startup Checklist*, 99.

2 Michael McQueen, "QuickBooks Connect Keynote Presentation in San Jose," YouTube video, posted December 11, 2019, 27:10, youtube .com/watch?v=hUNM8svEvgU.

Appendix 3: Milestones

1 Caelan Huntress, "My Favourite Quote of All Time Is a Misattribution," Medium, August 24, 2017, medium.com/the-mission/my-favourite -quote-of-all-time-is-a-misattribution-66356f22843d.

2 McQueen, "QuickBooks Connect Keynote Presentation."

Index

About the Author

T ATIANA TSOIR IS a visionary accountant, CEO, and founder of Linza Advisors Inc. She is a numbers expert who helps entrepreneurs and business owners become the boss of their bottom line. As the host of the popular podcast *Talk to Tatiana*, Tsoir reaches national and international audiences with her virtual trainings, talks, and writing about the simple, actionable steps for knowing your numbers, getting taxes under control, and reducing money anxiety. She helps clients around the world gain confidence and avoid costly money mistakes so that they can earn more doing what they love.

Learn more about Tatiana and her programs at **tatianatsoir.com** and **dreamboldbook.com**.